RISE **ABOVE**

A CHICAGO SUCCESS STORY

WRITTEN BY JEFF DASE

Dr. Kennedy,
    Thank you for the support. Great
meeting you and look forward to
the continued networking.
                                    Jeff Dase

CONTENTS

INTRODUCTION

About the Author

I was born and raised on the city of Chicago's south side. I lived in an urban area known as Roseland until my mother and father moved our family to another part of the south side known as Washington Heights. I attended elementary and high school in Chicago, which has the third largest public school district in America. I went on to earn a Bachelor's of Science in Elementary Education degree from Chicago State University on a full academic scholarship. After earning my Bachelor's degree, I became an elementary school teacher for Chicago Public Schools. While teaching, I earned a Masters of Art in General Administration degree from Chicago State University. I would teach, coach and mentor at the elementary level for six years before becoming an assistant principal at the high school level for four years. I've been fortunate to be able to serve students as a principal and then as the Chief of Schools for one the Chicago Public Schools' regional networks.

I have served on consultancy groups and task forces aimed at improving overall systems and structures that lead to student and school success. With the many hats that I have worn, the one constant has been mentoring students, especially the black male students. As you will read throughout the book, from my days as a school tutor to my current position, I have always found time to develop and implement a black male mentoring structure into my work as an educational professional. My efforts have provided foundation and structure for numerous success stories. One of my students earned the Bill Gates Millennium Scholarship which provided funding for his post-secondary studies. I have been a catalyst for providing internship opportunities for students that have led to full-time, lucrative employment for inner city urban youth. I have made sacrifices so the next generation will have better opportunities and chances to become better productive citizens than the ones before them, including me.

I was inspired to write this book because I feel a lot of people, young and not so young, have issues related to the concepts I'll be discussing, but do not have an outlet to express or talk about them. I too have held a lot of issues in throughout my lifetime and wanted to write this book as a tool to get people to open up and discuss. Many people look at me as a successful black male, which I feel comes off the wrong way at times, as I'll explain later in this book. I am a successful man who embraces my blackness as an enhancement that makes me even more dynamic. I am a successful man who has dealt with and is still dealing with misfortune and other issues that could have derailed my success at numerous times as a child, adolescent and adult. I want this book to be a conversation starter. The first step to improvement is to get it out and talk about it, so here I go.

My original title was "From Church Street to the Chief Seat" but I decided "Rise Above" would be more fitting. Read and let me know your thoughts.

CHAPTER 1

Make a Decision, Mother or Father

As a six-year-old male, I was presented with a critical thinking situation early in life. How I approached the situation ultimately had a lasting impact on my entire life as a man. As I look back, that situation actually impacted my professional life just as much as my personal life.

My mother and father were arguing in the front room. This wasn't the first time I heard my mother and father fighting but it was the first time the argument would turn physical. My mother picked up a vase and threw it at my father hitting him in the head causing a deep gash and trickles of blood that terrified me.

As this story illustrates, my mother was the aggressive one from that partnership. My father was always mild-mannered. My mother and father did not ever marry but co-habitated during my childhood. It was me, my mother, my father, my sister and my cousin, whom I

4

call my sister. Both of my parents worked while I was growing up. My mother worked for an air conditioning and heating company while my father worked for a plating company which made nuts and bolts. First, we lived in a single-floor apartment on the second floor of an apartment building in Roseland. It was a family building, meaning the tenants in the other two apartments were family also. If we were poor, we didn't know we were poor because I remember good times at that apartment building. Later we moved into a house, and then we became one of the first families from there to move into the nicer Washington Heights neighborhood.

Moving to Washington Heights meant moving near better schools and better living arrangements. We would now have a front porch, front lawn and back lawn. My mother still lives in the same house today so as you can see, we are a family that doesn't like a lot of change.

Getting back to the critical thinking problem that would ultimately impact my life. As I watched my father bleeding from the head, my mother was shouting at him to get out and pushing him out the door. What occurred next will remain with me always. My father looked back at my mother and said, "Give me my son!"

In the midst of my crying I started walking towards my father and my mother told me "Get your ass back in that room." I stopped in my steps. My father finally left and my mother closed the door and walked by me without saying another word. She is upset and crying. After what seemed like an eternity (but probably was only about two minutes), I jumped on the front room couch, opened the green curtains and saw my father sitting on the front porch, still bleeding from the head. I still don't know what made me do what I did next, but I hopped down off the couch and unlocked the front door. Pulling it open, I said "Daddy" and that is when my father grabbed me and we started walking down the street. We walked from 105th Street to 109th street. It wasn't a straight shot so we had to walk over 2 miles to my Aunt Annie Ruth's house. Now I say we walked but actually my father had put me on his back the entire way while still bleeding from the head.

We entered my aunt's garden apartment. My father sat me on the couch as my aunt began to give my father first aid. We stayed at my aunt's house for a couple of days before I returned back home with my mother. My father wouldn't ever live with us again. That night would have a lasting impression on my life. I chose to go with my father that night and my father and I have been like best friends ever since. Well, friends don't beat you with leather belts like my father did at times but you know what I mean. I have always looked up to my father and wanted to be like him, a hard worker who knows how to enjoy life. My father never had a lucrative job but he made me feel like I was rich because he always provided for me. Now, he would cut corners, like if I wanted or needed some new shoes, he would buy the imitations in my early years until my friends started clowning me in elementary school. I probably was in sixth grade before getting my first name brand gym shoes which were the black and white All-Star Converse worn by my childhood idol, Larry Bird of the Boston Celtics.

That night impacted my life for years to come as my relationship with my daughter mirrors the relationship I have with my father. My father was a man that always looked out for me and I try to do the same for the young males I interact with every day in my personal and professional life. My father made sacrifices and wanted better for me and I am making sacrifices for my daughter and youth daily to have a better life than me. I haven't been physically wounded but I take psychological blows daily for students in an attempt to give them better.

When I returned home, my mother did not reference the night. It was as if the situation did not happen and there were new arrangements, let's move on. So it seemed! One Sunday, not long after when I returned home, I was being lazy about going to church. I often tell people my mother gave me a "drug" problem when I was young. She "drug" me to church every Sunday whether I liked it or not. So on this particular Sunday, my mother wasn't having it so to motivate me, she gave me a whipping and while she was whipping me she added "And yeah, this for you opening that door and leaving with your daddy." Although delayed, I did get reprimanded for my critical thinking problem solving skills. My mother is a no-nonsense female. She catered to my sister as I was growing up, and I didn't understand until later that this was because my sister required more as she was the black sheep of the family. I always admired my mother for taking in my cousin also known to me as my big sister when her mother died. At a very young age, I realized my mother had a huge heart and a lot on her so I always tried to stay out of trouble so I would not disrupt her schedule. I tried, and most of the time I was successful.

My father and I would be together every weekend. He would move from apartment to apartment throughout the years and finally landed a two-bedroom unit where I had my own bedroom. He would often pick me up after work on Friday. He would have Jay's plain potato chips, a Hostess cupcake and Pepsi for me. We would spend the weekend together which included him cooking; most often, it was pork chops and a salad with French dressing.

My father struggled sometimes between balancing the bachelor life and being a single parent but overall, he did a great job. He would drop me off at family member's houses, often on the west side, when he went to see his girlfriend. Most of my cousins were either too old or too young for me to hang with or play with so I often ended up watching television while eating McDonald's. I would make friends in the neighborhood but most of the time I would just wait patiently for my father to return. Those experiences taught me patience at a young age. Even if I wasn't with my father, I *was* with him because I knew he was coming back to pick me up. I did not ever want to disappoint my parents so I tried hard to make them proud. That is the same relationship I try to build with my students and youth I mentor. When you can get them to the point where they don't want to disappoint you, they will work hard to please you and ultimately be successful. The same approach also works for adults.

Another critical thinking decision I made was as an adolescent. Throughout my childhood, I wanted my last name changed to reflect my true family bloodline, which is Hayes. Only a few people know that the name Dase is from my sister's father, not my father. For some reason that still has not been disclosed, I was given my sister's father name instead of my father's name at birth. My mother and my sister's father was married and divorced before my mother and father became a couple. I resented the name growing up but quickly realized it was working in my favor as I grew up applying for jobs with my friends. I would always get calls back and my friends would rarely. I attributed it to the employers' inability to identify my race by my name Dase. By the time I would complete the interview, they could see I was a nice young man and would offer me the job. I would also help with their diversity statistics as well but many of my friends would be discriminated against from their names. I was given the opportunity to showcase myself when my friends would not even get to the door. When this continued, I decided to keep the name Dase. So when I come down on people for giving their babies crazy first names, I am dead serious. It's not fair to close doors for a life at birth. The name game is real. Give them a chance to have all doors open so they can showcase their greatness like I was able to do.

Overall, I had a great childhood. I grew up in a part of town known as the Wild Hundreds, in a house with a big back yard. I had friends and I attended a nice school, both elementary and high school. I was able to roam the neighborhood with my friends and by myself. We had a neighborhood park in walking distance. When I think about the current violence in Chicago neighborhoods, I really see how blessed we were growing up. Sure, we had our share of violence but nothing on an on-going basis like you hear about and witness today.

The Wild Hundreds had its rough sides also; some were with gangs that demonstrated under the five point star like the Vice Lords, others demonstrated under the six point star like the Gangster Disciples. You also had the Four Corner Hustlers that demonstrated under the four point star. The Latin Kings were also a neighborhood gang in the Wild Hundreds. I grew up on 105th and Church Street which was land of the Vice Lords. My family, however, was all Gangster Disciples. I learned at an early age how to navigate between the two groups. My neighborhood family respected me enough to respect my immediate family when they would come over and visit. They knew my immediate family was from a rival gang but there was not ever any conflict when they would come visit and attend family functions at my mother's house. As you will read later in this book, navigating between these two groups would become lifelong.

I can remember playing for the neighborhood, Graver Park basketball team during elementary school. Once, we had a game scheduled at Edward White Park in another part of the Wild Hundreds, which was all Gangster Disciples. As we arrived at White Park, we saw the Gangster Disciples blocking the entrance to the park. Everybody on the bus was damn-near scared out of our basketball shoes then I noticed someone I knew. I knew the leader from that neighborhood. They called him Trouble. I knew Trouble because he hung with my cousin Calvin and I would kick it with them whenever I would go see Calvin on weekends. Once I saw Trouble, I knew we were all good but I didn't tell my friends. I acted like the big shot and said, I got this, let me off the bus. All my friends were looking like this Negro crazy.

When I got to the group blocking the entrance, I said, "What's up Trouble!" He said, "Aw, that's Lil Cook, what's up man." He told the group of Gangster Disciples to let us in and the entire group dispersed. I looked back and told my friends to come on. My friends treated me like a king that evening and kept asking me how you do that. I didn't ever tell them the truth but we had several more games at White Park and no one would go without me. I guess I have been good at keeping secrets for a long time. As I said, I learned at an early age to navigate between the groups of gangs.

Another time, we were playing basketball in the Wild Hundreds and, again, in Gangster Disciples territory. We had been playing what seemed like all day when my friends and I were walking across the bridge back to our part of town and here comes a group of GDs from behind us, yelling GD. They knew most of my friends were Vice Lords. Back in the day, basketball was a neutralizer to gang violence. We would play and beat rival gangs and live to brag about it. I'm not so sure if it would go down like that these days, especially in Chicago. So all my friends run and not that I was the bravest of us all, I was just too damn tired to run on this day. I can remember the leader on the bike muffing me in the head while I kept walking. They could have beaten the hell out of me if they wanted but they just wanted to scare us. It worked overall but I was just too tired to run on this day. I received mad love when I got back to the block for not running. I would not ever run from a situation again.

I like to say the Lord has been with me all my life because it was several situations that could have turned out bad but did not. That was one of them. Another thing that was different when I grew up in Chicago was that we fought with our fists instead of with guns. You might get a broken rib or hand but you lived to learn and see another day unlike today. I once saw a fight last for over one hour as the two took breaks and continued. It was like a heavyweight street fight. One did have to go to the hospital as result, but at least he avoided the tragic outcomes we see with gun violence. Not only have guns ruined lives but they ruined a lot of fun for us growing up as well. Almost all our fun spots closed due to gun violence that led to a slow decline and eventual death of venues like the Halsted Drive-In Movie Theater, the go-carts, roller skating rink, park district basketball courts just to name a few. Today's generation may have more technology and resources, but my generation had more fun in my opinion. We were forced to use our creative thinking to have fun with much less, but we did it and had positive enjoyment along the way. My childhood and adolescent years were not perfect by far but they prepared me for life and gave me an appreciation for life.

Although they were separated, my mother and father put me in a great situation early in life to be successful yet ultimately be a kid. I will forever be grateful to them for their sacrifices.

CHAPTER 2

Family Love, The Abuse

As a male in a household of women, no matter how young you are, you are sometimes considered the man of the house. This can bring an unwanted burden on a young male who just wants to be a kid and grow up normal. I was that kid. A true introvert that was comfortable playing by myself, doing things by myself and even talking to myself. I use to play full court basketball games by myself in my second floor bedroom. I would place a tin garbage can at each end of my bedroom and play certain players on each team throughout the game. The games were timed. I had half time and there were a lot of outstanding buzzer beaters. When there would be a hard foul, my mother would yell up the stairs, boy, what are you doing up there? I kept statistics, which is probably why I was always good in calculations and statistics throughout school. I would have a playoff bracket where east and west teams would compete against each other for the championship. I played a   full NBA (National

Basketball Association) season played by myself, all I needed was two tin garbage cans, and a soft miniature size basketball.

The introvert activities didn't stop there. I also played full MLB (Major League Baseball) seasons as well in the back yard with an old kitchen chair as the strike out box. The back of the old kitchen chair served as the strike out zone and if I didn't throw three strikes before four balls the imaginary runner would advance around the bases. You can only imagine the games were extremely long but also extremely exciting to me. I could have become a professional pitcher with all the pitches I threw but baseball was not ever one of my favorite sports to play. I know if you are reading this, you are wondering what the hell was wrong with me and you probably are wondering what about football. Well football was extremely hard to play with just one person but I tried but ultimately I played my football seasons on my electric football game that allowed you to march football action figures down the vibrating football field. I also loved the Tecmo Bowl football game on the Nintendo game system which I completed full seasons playing with also. I rotated between the Houston Oilers and Los Angeles Raiders. I would score at will with the Run and Shoot offense of Houston or run over everybody with the Raiders' Bo Jackson.

So, as you can imagine, I was a loner, a true introvert who created amazing events by myself and with myself. As a young male, I was always taught not to hit a female. I'm proud I'm able to say I have not ever violated those parental directives that I live by to this day. One day, my sister, my cousin, and I were just sitting around talking. I don't remember what sparked the conversation but the topic was who could beat who, me or my sister. I reminded them that men, me being a young man at the time, don't hit girls. My sister started saying I'm just scared and that she would beat me. I started to walk away, and she surprised me by beginning to pummel me with her fist, letting her fingernails do some of the work. My cousin intervened and I went down the stairs crying, not knowing what had just happened; that moment would be the beginning of a miserable chapter in my life.

My sister would mistreat and abuse me in so many different ways for the next year but it seemed like a lifetime. We were latchkey kids, meaning we had keys to the house and were to come straight home after school, do our homework and if we were able to complete without my mother's assistance we could go out and play in the neighborhood until the street lights came on. My mother would get home every day at 4 o'clock. On a normal day, I would leave school at 2:30 p.m., get home by 3:00 p.m. to watch *The Flintstones* and , *The Jetsons* , do my homework and then go out and play with my friends. After my sister discovered I wouldn't hit her back, she would make sure to get home before me, lock the screen door which had no key lock and make sure I stayed outside until she unlocked the screen door at 4:00 p.m., right before my mother would come home. Initially, I would tell my mother and she would simply tell my sister to stop it. The mistreatment continued and I would simply stay outside and play until my mother came home even though I missed watching cartoons. It became hard when it was raining or during the winter months when no friends were out playing and I'm outside in the rain or cold alone. I would wait under the back porch until my mother's car pulled up and hear the screen door unlatch and go into the house. I became immune to the mistreatment. One day to my surprise, the screen door was not locked. I started smiling and went inside to watch cartoons. I went into the house, fixed me a bowl of Frosted Flakes and laid across my bed watching *The Flintstones*. Suddenly, my sister entered my bedroom and without warning, smacked me in the face. She smacked me so hard, the cereal and my body hit the floor. She began to beat me in my back as I was trying to cover up and then just left the room. That was mild compared to what was coming in the future.

One time, she ripped my shirt off my back and begins to rack her fingernails across my back as I hollered out "Stop!" I remembered looking in the bathroom mirror and seeing tracks of blood down my back as I cried out why me? Why am I going through this? The mistreatment and beatings would continue for a long period of time. Through it all, I did not once hit my sister back. I took every last hit. As I said previously, my sister is the black sheep of the family and she stayed in trouble during her adolescent years. My mother is one of those parents who believes in the saying "I brought you in this world and I'll take you out." One night after another defiant episode from my sister, my mother almost brought those words to life. I almost lost both my sister and mother in one night. I don't remember what my sister did but ████████████████████████████ ████████████████████████████████ the result was ████████████████████ my sister being removed from our house by DCFS (Department of Children and Family Services).

This would begin my sister's path in and out of foster homes and the juvenile justice system. This would also begin my peace as a young man and adolescent. My sister never returned to live with us as a family throughout her teenage years. Whenever we would visit or she would come to visit, there would be drama. I eventually stopped going to visit and my mother respected my stance.

The mistreatment and abuse I endured from the hands of my own blood sister is why I have difficulty trusting people. It is also why I believe in right and wrong, regardless of bloodline. Deep down, I had some resentment towards my mother for not stopping the abuse and catering to my sister more than me but again, I realized later, my sister needed more attention. I developed trust issues with my mother that I will reveal later. I had to face reality that the trauma I endured from my sister really messed my head and heart up.

Years passed and my sister resurfaced. By this time I had graduated from college twice. My mother solicited support from the family to help my sister move to Mississippi because she continued to get into trouble in Chicago. At this time, I was an assistant principal, and because I didn't want my sister's presence to burden my mother, I covered the expenses to move my sister to Mississippi. I had forgiven my sister's misdeeds against me but I did not forget. I will never forget. So we moved my sister to Mississippi. She acquired a home from the government assistance program and was living great. Key word - was. After about a year, my sister was back to her criminal behavior and had to immediately move from Mississippi due to a warrant for her arrest. By this time, I could see this was not going to end well so I tell my mother I wasn't giving another dime to my sister and that they could let her trap them into the drama if they wanted. I'm done.

While she was back in Chicago, she stole from my mother, got arrested multiple times and was back on drugs. She even came to my job with a group of hypes (persons under the influence of drugs) demanding money. I eventually had to pay my own sister off to stop her from harassing me on my job, my nice city job.

Years passed and again we didn't hear too much from my sister except occasionally when she would call to get bailed out of jail. One Christmas my mother invited my sister over. A family friend came over. The family friend helps my mother often. Everyone was talking in the family room. I was in the television room watching the basketball game. Suddenly, I heard my sister cursing out the family friend. She was jealous of the relationship my mother and the family friend had. The family friend left and my mother attempted to calm my sister down. As my sister walked past me she begins to curse at me, telling me "you ain't shit, I'll fuck you up too." She opened the utensil drawer in the kitchen, got one of the largest knives in the drawer, and came towards me. I dodged the first swing. My mother got in between us and pushed my sister back. My daughter was witnessing this and began crying.

Police were dispatched to my mother's house. My daughter couldn't stop crying. I looked at my mother without having to say anything. I filed a restraining order against my sister. I told her, "I see now I cannot be around you. If you come right, I'm going left." That was the last day I saw my sister; those were the last words I spoke to my sister. It's been over five years now with no interactions with my sister. I'm at peace. The last interaction with my sister, I saw my life flash before my eyes because I wanted to kill her. Here I had endured years of mistreatment and abuse; I had provided her money to get her life and affairs together and she still wanted to pull a knife on me, possibly kill me. My sister is the closest thing to the devil I have ever experienced. Sometimes, to keep or enjoy your blessings you have to run from others.. I'm running from my sister. I will see her

after her judgment day, if then.

CHAPTER 3

Disappointments Lead to Success

Even though you have to love life, you also have to know that it is full of disappointments. I call disappointments tests, they test your will to persevere. They test what you are really made of. Disappointments are a part of life, but how you handle disappointments can be the difference between life and death. I'm what most would consider a successful black man. As I stated earlier, I feel that statement in itself is disrespectful because it's saying I'm only successful from the measure of a black man or your expectations of a black man. I say I'm a successful man that happens to be black and proud. My education, experience and accomplishments stand up to all men, black, brown or white. I often tell young men that I mentor who mostly are black, don't limit your expectations to what only black men do, and instead compete on a national and global level with all colors, races and ethnic groups. Disappointments and failures can breed success and the earlier in life you experience disappointments the better, in my opinion.

Childhood and adolescence are the training grounds when you are given multiple chances to get it right or screw it up. Adulthood is not so understanding. I have seen students curse out their teacher, get a parent conference and sometimes a suspension and return in a few days to the same environment. When you are an adult and you curse out your boss, you get fired. PERIOD. GAME OVER. This is why I always preach schools need to teach life skills. How students engage in a school setting is totally different, in most cases, than what is acceptable in the real world.

I was recently the keynote speaker at a summer school eighth grade graduation. These students did not meet the requirements to graduate with their peers in June and had to attend summer school. Basically, they received a second chance. I told them that not graduating in June was a disappointment, not a failure, but that how they handled the disappointment will make them better students in high school. They could have easily remained upset and not attended summer school. They would then have had to repeat eighth grade which would have been an official failure. It took heart and commitment to go to summer school while your friends were out playing or on summer vacations. I told them, I bet it will not happen again because they know the feeling.

That disappointment will lead to success for those students. Speaking of disappointments, I told the graduates, I too had to attend summer school to advance to the next grade level; mine happened in third grade so I knew the feeling and passed eighth grade on the honor roll. My earlier disappointments led to my elementary school success. Not only did I graduate on the honor roll but I was one of the lead vocalist at the eighth grade graduation along with my best friend Corey, rest in peace. Corey Knox and I led *"Wind Beneath My Wings"* at the 1989 Alice L. Barnard commencement ceremony.

Speaking of elementary school, it was very different back in the 1980's from today. For one, we were actually allowed to go home for lunch and return on our own. That is unheard of today at the elementary school level. It shows how much the world has changed as it relates to safety and overall values of society. I had some great times in elementary school. I had some great friends and great teachers as well. I still keep in touch with some of these friends to this day, like Mike Brown, Demon Wilson and Julius Scott. Julius and I battle a lot over sports as he is a diehard Chicago fan and I don't like any Chicago teams. I get together annually with Demon as he does a back-to-school supply drive for the kids in his neighborhood each summer before they go back to school. I also had great teachers in elementary school. When I was promoted to Chief of Schools, two of my teachers reached out to me to say congratulations and took me to lunch, Teresa Connell and Albert Chaps. They cared then and continue to care now. That's genuine support and encouragement. Throughout elementary school, I received good grades and played sports, mostly basketball. I was the starting small forward my eighth grade year which was a highlight. We went to the championship my seventh grade year and lost by one point. That was a dynamic team that year, led mostly by players besides me at the time but I enjoyed learning from them as I mostly rode the bench. If you ask me, I also had the best looking girlfriend in elementary school also, Simone Wilson. I was too young to even engage properly with a girl then; hell, it took me two years just to kiss her. When we finally kissed one Sunday afternoon at Graver Park, I thought I'd lost my mind and it was a dream. We would kiss often after that. I guess I owe her for giving me practice and sharpening my kissing skills.

Parents need to really pay attention and be aware of where their children are and who they are with. My parents did not pay too much attention to where I was at and who I was with as long as nothing happened that brought attention to a certain situation. Being a dad and growing up under the influence that I did, I was always cautious of where Jakia was and who she was with as much as I could. That's for these parents that often say "Not my baby." Yeah, "your baby" is out there doing things that you don't even know about. Overall, elementary school years were fun. We were able to be kids and explore life without many boundaries and we handled it well considering.

Another disappointment I experienced in elementary school was during the high school selection process. Our neighborhood high school was Morgan Park High School but due to limited seats, they had a lottery system. All my friends from elementary school that lived in the neighborhood won the chance to attend Morgan Park. My best friend Corey lived two houses from me and was selected and I was not. I was projected to attend Fenger High School, which was two miles away from my house and a two bus ride trip.

My mother was not accepting the placement and went to the Board of Education. I don't know exactly what she said but they gave her the option of enrolling me into Percy L. Julian High School the following school year. This was an unprecedented move by my mother because she was pretty much hands off with my education-- I was relatively a good student and she worked a lot. My mother really stepped up then and it would prove to be a decision that would have a lasting positive impact on my life overall. I would be the only one from my neighborhood to attend Percy Lavon Julian High School. God is great because he placed me at a school where I would acquire a great education amongst caring leaders and competitive students that pushed me to reach my full potential often. Julian High School was a competitive environment that produced a lot of successful individuals. I met some of my close friends there, like Rodney White-El who still cuts my hair to this day despite cutting my tail off in High School. My best friend, Clarence Clair would attend Julian High School as well. I met Clarence during my eighth grade year. His stepdad and my dad knew each other. My dad lived close to them at the time, and one Saturday, me and Clarence met and started talking and we were cool with each other ever since. We didn't know each other was planning on attending Julian but we saw each other in the hallway during the first week of our freshmen year. Our relationship grew in high school to the point we became best friends. If you saw me, Clarence was nearby. If you saw Clarence, I was nearby. We both were a part of one of the many Julian social clubs called F.L.I.P.P which was an acronym for _____ _____ _____ _____ _____. We had majority of the females at Julian High School. The Phi Dogs, Bruhz and PJ Players may say differently but, hey, this my book. Clarence and I were so close that during our senior year when friends solicited both of us to run for Prom King, Clarence dropped out of the competition which is probably why I ended up winning and being named Prom King in 1993. That was an example of how he looked out for me in high school and still does to this day. It's hard to find genuine friends and friendship of that magnitude but ours survived and increased throughout our 30 years of knowing each other. Besides Clarence, I developed life-long friends at Julian High School that I still keep in contact with to this day. Julian High School was the college experience before college. We had pride back then and still do to this day.

Fast forward to my sophomore year in high school. While I was going to Julian, I still hung out with friends from the neighborhood. On Feb. 1, 1991, we were celebrating the birthday of Simone, rest in peace. I'm not sure what we were all drinking but I know one item in the circle was Night Train wine. Night Train Express to be exact. We were mixing drinks and talking smack to one another for at least two hours all while outside in the back of Steve's garage. Not sure who, but some genius from the group made the decision to walk up to Western Avenue. That meant we had to walk through the heart of the Beverly neighborhood which was mostly whites. Just imagine, a group of intoxicated young black males walking a mile through a mostly white neighborhood. This was not going to turn out well. All I remember is us drinking behind Steve's garage, and then waking up as the police are dragging me and my other friends out of Princeton's bedroom closet. The police officers drove us to Little Caesar's Pizza on Western Avenue, and yanked us out the squad car by the hand cuffs on our hands. They stood all three of us up and one by one ask, is this him? When they point to me, the female employee behind the counter says yes, that's him. They put us back in the squad car, took us to the police station and began processing us and calling our parents. While this is going on, my insides succumb to all the alcohol and I throw up on the police station floor. Next thing I remember is my mother's and father's faces of shame.

The police allowed them to take me home because I was extremely intoxicated otherwise they were going to take me to the juvenile detention center that night. I woke up the next morning with a headache, my first hangover and scars on both of my hands. The police handcuffs had left deep cuts in my hands from the police dragging me by them. My mother entered my bedroom, still with a shameful face and informed me I have a court date and they have to get a lawyer because the Little Caesar's employee accused me of a crime. Days turned into weeks. Weeks turned into months. Months turned into a year. February 1, 1991 was the last day I hung with my friends from the neighborhood until well after my college years. I didn't blame my friends but I knew I had to separate myself to stay focused. I knew I did not ever want to see that look on my mother's face again. I had deeply disappointed her and I was committed to making it right. I went to court, but the accuser did not show. We were all excited and the judge continued the case giving the accuser an opportunity to show up at the next court date. I have not ever seen my father so upset but he had to take it or risk jeopardizing my freedom. We attended the next court date, the accuser did not show and the case was dismissed. To this day, I don't know exactly what happened but my friends say my friend Ricardo reached to see the female employee name badge and touched her. They said they still don't know why she identified me because me and Ricardo look nothing alike. February 1, 1991 was a turning point in my life and I haven't been in any trouble since. Well ...

I graduated from Percy Lavon Julian High School in 1993 and went on to attend Chicago State University. During my junior year in high school, I'd joined Future Teachers of Chicago, a group for those students interested in going into the teaching profession. At the time, I was not interested in becoming a teacher. I was interested in the females in the group. It was only one other male student in the group. The group also participated in a lot of field trips which I liked as well. During my senior year, most of my friends were making post-secondary decisions and I was still undecided. This was back in the day when schools had the scared straight approach and were telling us, particularly young black males, we were going to be dead or in jail and for us to get our act together which meant get a job or go to school after high school. I knew dead and jail were not options for me so I started looking into the armed forces. I just wanted to be off the streets and for my parents not to have to go in debt for my college education.

After more discussion, I decided to sign up for the Army. I passed my exams and they told me where I would be stationed and the final step was the weigh in. At the weigh in, I was seven pounds under weight. At that point, my recruiter told me to eat potatoes and bananas the following week to put on more weight. As I'm eating potatoes and bananas to put on more weight the following week, I get a letter in the mail from Chicago State University. The letter says Congratulations, you are the recipient of a full-scholarship to Chicago State University. That letter granted me my wishes, my parents would not have to go in debt for my college education and I would be off the streets obtaining a degree from Chicago State University, for free, that's the best part.

I would go on to attend Chicago State University. Not only would I receive the full academic scholarship to go into education but I would also receive the Monetary Award Program (MAP)

Scholarship for students' assistance along with other financial aid assistance. Attending college was like winning the lottery for me. I have always been good with money management but with all this surplus of money, I decided to invest in the stock market. This was during the time when technology stocks took the stock market to record limits so needless to say, I made money also. I always tell students my college financial aid story when they say education does not pay. Attending college on a full academic scholarship allowed me to bank all other financial aid I qualified for. Unlike most young adults, who like the bling bling and things that depreciate in value, I invested my money in things that appreciated in value, particularly stocks and savings bonds. I was fortunate enough to have a conversation with my friend Vincent who worked for a bank at the time about the stock market and how it could increase your wealth. From the money I made investing, I was able to buy my first car without a co-signer, save up for a down payment on my first home, which was in a sought-after neighborhood of Chicago, and pay for my tuition when I pursued and completed my Master's degree at

Chicago State University. I acquired Bachelor's and Master's Degrees debt free.

Not only did that investment pay for my education, but I saved enough to assist with my daughter's post-secondary education as well. She would go on to graduate from Northern Illinois University. You will read more about that in an upcoming chapter. Not only did I invest in the stock market, which was booming at the time, but Vincent also told me about investing in savings bonds. He told me that if I bought a $25 savings bond and held it for a while, I could redeem if for $50 later. I thought that was a no-brainer so every paycheck I would buy a $25 savings bond. I eventually moved up to buying $50, $100 and $300 savings bonds that I still haven't cashed in but each one has doubled in value. I bought them in case I needed money down the line in life. Luckily, I haven't had to cash them in for an emergency but I'm about to cash them in soon because they have stopped accumulating cash value. All this was possible from me continuing my education beyond high school. Education does pay. Education pays well.

Besides becoming financially stable and literate, college was fun as hell. I was a black male in the field of education which is dominated by females. I would attend class and often be the only male in the classroom which was great! I met some of my closest friends in college. We had a group of four that banded together through thick and thin, good and bad. It was myself, Juwana, Janice and Ariana. We took classes together, knew each other families, and had fun together and all graduated together. I contribute my college success to our group and friendship. The work seemed easy and fun as we completed it together. I would recommend that approach to any student during their post-secondary journey. I took the same approach when acquiring my Master's degree only this time it was Carol and Deborah, my two big sisters. They both were older than me but had young spirits and energy. They call me their little brother. Our study sessions were the best and we always had great food. We all knew each other families and still today get together and keep in touch. Everyone from all my college groups was at my daughter's trunk party and they have continued to support me throughout my life and career. I always say, I didn't get this far by myself. I am grateful for a lot of people for their support, love and patience with me.

I went on to graduate with a Bachelor's of Science degree in Elementary Education. I would return one year later to pursue and eventually finish with a Masters of Arts in General Administration degree from Chicago State University also. I immediately knew Education Pays.

College days were not without their disappointments. During my last year of college, I would break up with my daughter's mother. This was a devastating experience for me because I just knew we would be the husband and wife and everything nice couple. It hit me hard because I had invested a lot of time and money into building our family. We had been together since high school and I had not ever gone through a relationship break up of this magnitude. The break up also put a strain on our families. Both our families became close as we were together. Not only were our immediate families close but we found out during our relationship that our extended

42

families knew each other as well. Her west side extended family knew my west side extended family. We had a lot of people cheering us on for a bright future.

One day, towards the closure of our relationship, I became upset at some alarming information and she and her brother thought I was going to harm her so as I'm approaching the back door of her mother's house at the time, I encountered her young brother near the garage. The next thing I know, I was staring down the barrel of a sawed-off shot gun. At that moment, I was filled with so much anger, I don't remember being scared but in looking back I was one trigger from being dead at the hands of my soon to be brother- in-law. We had a stare down with brief comments before I would leave and drive off. Our relationship would not ever be the same since then but I still got love for the dude.

My daughter's mother had several cousins and extended family members that were cool people so the break up wasn't just us two not being together but a lot of people that became distant. Ultimately

I had to cope and maintain my focus on acquiring my degree, which I did. Along the way family members had major disputes which turned violent, domestic issues surfaced and as mentioned previously, trust issues surfaced between me and my mother. My mother loves my daughter's mother and was on her side more than mine at times and there were things said that didn't sit well with me as a son coming from my mother. My daughter's mother and I had a strained relationship for some years but the separation from her also built my resilience and ability to adjust to hard times and stay focused because that's what the world requires. The world does not care about your personal problems. You have to stay focused or risk losing what you worked for. It all worked out. Today my daughter's mother and I are close friends. She's married to a wonderful husband who loves my daughter--I can't ask for much more. The disappointments of a broken relationship led to two individuals setting aside differences to raise a successful young lady, Jakia Janay Dase.

CHAPTER 4

A New Birth Yields a Renewed Focus

In my final year at Chicago State University, I was recruited by Dallas Public School system to teach science. The offer was lucrative at the time. They offered to move me down to Dallas and pay for my moving expenses. Upon discussing with my daughter's mother, I decided not to take the offer because she was against moving my daughter out of state and I was against moving without my daughter. In hindsight, everything worked out for the best anyway, but lessons learned; actions of today may impact decisions tomorrow. Had I not had my daughter I would have definitely accepted the Dallas offer and moved away from Chicago. 21 years later, I'm still here in Chicago and loving my life. God is great.

Coming out of high school, while most of my friends were enjoying times as a fresh high school graduate, I was "caking" better known as with my girlfriend Tracey too much. I'm one that likes and loves hard which has been a good and bad thing throughout my life. Back then, I was madly in love with Tracey and just thought spending every moment with her was the right thing to do. It wasn't all that bad but I did miss out on some experiences just growing up into adulthood. I can remember many conversations with my best friend Clarence about being with her too much and neglecting my other friends. Don't get me wrong, Clarence loved Tracey but he recognized that we only get certain parts of our lives to live it up and being fresh out of high school is one of those times in life. Well, when you are a young man, full of testosterone, what are you doing frequent? In my case it was ███████████████████

███████████████████████████████████

███████████████████████████████████

███████████████████████████████████

███████████████████████████████████

███████████████████████████████████

███████████████████████████████████

███████████████████████████████████

███████████████████████████████████

███████████████████████████████████

██████████████████████████████████████

██████████████████████████████████████

██████████████████████████████████████

████████████████████ Again, the conversation and thoughts were stupid as hell. ██████████████████████████

██████████████████████████████████████

██████████████████████████████████████

████████ I guess I can blame Clarence for me getting Tracey pregnant and us having a child. If so, I guess I can thank Clarence for us having one of the best gifts God has ever given me, my daughter, Jakia Janay Dase. Jakia name actually derived from one of my high school girlfriend names but naturally, Tracey wasn't going to give her that exact name so we agreed to change the N to a J and we had Jakia. Janay came because I was unsure if Jakia would be a marketable name when it came down to getting a job so I wanted to give her a universal name that people would not use to discriminate against her so we decided on Janay. If Jakia became an obstacle in the future, she could just use Janay Dase. I was proud she had my last name, which really isn't my last name, but she would identify with me even though her mother and I wasn't married. I remember the night she was born like it was yesterday because it was comical. Her mother kicked me out of the delivery room in favor of her mother because I kept cracking jokes and she was not in a good mood. She was in labor for a long time. Jakia was born before midnight on December 24, 1995. She was almost a Christmas baby. I immediately felt an obligation to be a better person because I was responsible for another person now. My entire goal in life was to ensure my child had a better life than me and I had a great upbringing from my parents. I wanted to do this without spoiling her but it's kind of hard not to spoil an only child. It's not impossible however. I was still in college when Jakia was born. Her birth increased my drive to flourish and be a positive person in this world.

Whatever I did, I would always ask myself, would Jakia be proud of me for this or would I do this around Jakia? She was always a great kid. She had a jealous side when she was little but quickly grew out of that. I raised her like a man would raise a son at times. I would discourage her from crying. I had real- world conversations with her at an early age. I would be stern with her at times. The amazing part is she would take hold of lessons from me and make wise decisions throughout her life. She has a lot of my characteristics. That can be a good thing and a bad thing depending on who you talk to.

When I bought my first house, I made sure to have a classroom so I could support her academic development while she was with me. I would assign her a book or story passage to read and answer questions and several math worksheets every time she spent time with me. She would have to complete before playtime or any free time. We loved doing science projects together. Even though she didn't live with me, I supported her as if she did. If it meant driving to her mother's house after work, I did what I had to do to support my child. I tried to mirror our relationship after my relationship with my father. Although he didn't stay with me, I was not ever without a dad and my daughter will be able to say the same when she is older. I was there on every first day of school, parent-teacher conference, report card pick up and graduation.

Her mother was one of those mothers who felt her baby was a natural genius and pushed for Jakia to be moved up a grade in Pre-Kindergarten. I was against the idea but her mother made the decision so Jakia would not repeat Pre-Kindergarten instruction. I am an educator and I was more concerned about the maturity development at that age than academic preparedness. Jakia did well until second grade when she began to struggle a little. I remember having a conversation with her and threatening to place her in a school near me instead of the private school she was in. Again, her mother thought just because you paid for the education that it was better. Again, I disagreed and besides, I knew the educational system. I wanted to place Jakia in a public school where I knew the teachers were quality. Jakia's mother had convinced her public school was so bad that the simple threat of her attending a public school turned Jakia's drive around and she received good grades all the way through high school.

Jakia also was involved in various extracurricular activities while growing up. She was in dance, basketball and cheerleading. Those activities took up a lot of time. Dance class pretty much occupied my Saturdays and when she played AAU basketball that would occupy my Sundays. As I tell parents today, make the sacrifices now and you will not have to worry about them later. I also had the opportunity to coach biddy ball at the local park and Jakia was on my team. We won the biddy ball championship at Fernwood Park that year. That's one of the highlights of my life and as a dad.

When she graduated from high school I was able to give her one hundred dollars for each grade completed from Pre-Kindergarten through twelfth grade. She was discouraged during the college selection process. She had narrowed her choices down to the University of Kentucky and Northern Illinois University (NIU). Naturally, she and I took road trips to check out both universities. She was in love with the University of Kentucky. I felt it was more so of the sports program than academics. I was in love with Northern Illinois University more so for the in-state tuition. Both schools had solid Business programs which is the field she wanted to pursue. I remember taking her to breakfast and convincing her to attend

Northern Illinois University and then NIU sent her a letter declining her admission. She felt like if they don't want me, I'll go to University of Kentucky and prove them wrong, it's their loss. In my mind, I was like; no we are going to appeal the decision because you clearly qualify. I convinced her to file an appeal and they gave us an appeal meeting. This was one of the most cherished times of my life. Not only did I go to the meeting, but her mother and step-father, Ty attended the meeting as well. We went as united front for Jakia. The admissions representative said he would accept Jakia because he saw she had a supportive base that would serve her well throughout her years at NIU. Within 3 weeks, Jakia received an acceptance letter to NIU. We all moved her in, went to the University family events together and supported her throughout her four years at NIU. Jakia's drive amazed me throughout her years at NIU. She acquired a job at Target and would often call me on her way home from the library well after 11 o'clock at night. Her senior year, I paid for her to have an off campus apartment. She had a car to get around. She was developing into an outstanding independent young lady.

Jakia would graduate from NIU and once again, the supportive family that helped her get in was there on her graduation day. She was eager to move out on her own after graduation but once again, I would convince her otherwise. Her mother and stepdad would move to Virginia so I asked her to stay with me for at least one year while she saved her money to build so she would have a nice amount of money when she eventually moved out on her own. I also entered into an agreement with her that whatever she set aside for rent or mortgage for one year, I would match it up to one thousand dollars each month for one year. She will tell you there was no limit placed on the amount I would match. This was one of the best times of my life because although I had always been in Jakia's life, this would mark the first time we would come home to each other for an extended period of time longer than a weekend or school break.

During this year, we would discuss each other's work day, she would cook, and I would cook. We would spend time together and talk about time a part with friends. I offered to purchase her first condo or house. She decided against a house as her first living arrangements due to the space and maintenance. She also decided against me purchasing and acquired the home loan on her own. I advised her through the process and I was there when the deal was finalized but she basically did it all on her own. After acquiring a home loan, she negotiated a townhouse purchase on her own. Again, I advised and went on home viewings with her but she basically did on her own. I was there at the closing table as a proud dad once again.

At her house warming, I presented her with a check for twelve thousand dollars as she had set aside more than one thousand dollars a month for one year. She now resides on her own. We often have Saturday Daddy-Daughter dates in which we go to the movies and lunch. We take turns paying. She's officially an adult and I'm proud of her development. I could not have asked for a better child and overall life outcome. She's a Manager at Sherwin Williams Paint Company. It's so rewarding because the sacrifices paid off. All the missed outings, missed dates, girls being mad at me for the time I spent with my daughter, money spent ensuring her proper and appropriate development, it was all worth it. I would often pray that I would give up my great life in exchange for my daughter having a great life. I'm blessed the great Lord has made a way for us both to live a great life. Her birth brought me focus and increased my drive personally and professionally. I owe a lot of my success to the mere presence of my daughter, Jakia Janay Dase.

It's also important to know that although Jakia is my only birth daughter, I have another daughter, Breonna Green, from a previous relationship. I was with Breonna's mother for 6 years and with Breonna since she was twelve years old. We lived together. I was at her eighth grade, high school and college graduation. I have visited her in college at South Carolina State University where she was on a scholarship from running Track for Morgan Park High School. Once finished at South Carolina State University, I moved her out and back home to Chicago. Despite me and her mother not being together, we have stayed connected and have a father-daughter bond and connection. I have two daughters.

CHAPTER 5

Boys Make a Man

Fresh from finishing my student teacher assignment at Kohn Elementary School in the Roseland area of Chicago, I interviewed at Robert H. Lawrence Elementary school in the Jeffery Manor area of Chicago. I was sent to Lawrence by a Chicago Public Schools recruiter named John Thomas. The principal, William Harris, had a connection with John Thomas to send him any black male teachers with potential to his school. I guess John Thomas was the first person in Chicago Public Schools to recognize I had potential to be a great teacher. I arrived in an olive green suit that I purchased from the Evergreen Plaza. At the conclusion of the interview, Mr. Harris stated "you seem a little shy." I can't remember the comment after but I do remember him offering me the position to teach a second grade classroom before I left the school building. One of the questions was "Where do you see yourself in one to five years from now?" I replied that I wanted to pursue my Special Education certification and help students with special needs. My initial interest to pursue a special education certification was a result of recognizing the shortage of special education teachers and I knew with that certification I would always have a position in education. That shortage still exists today. I did not pursue my special education certification. Upon leaving the interview, the assistant principal walked me to the door and stated "look here, man; all these kids have special needs. We need more black males like you in administration. You should go get your administration certification."

I eventually enrolled in Chicago State University's General Administration Master Degree program to pursue my administration certification. Throughout my years as a teacher, my principal and assistant principal would give me encouragement and leadership opportunities that would prepare me to lead beyond the teacher position. That path was almost derailed after my first day on the job. I actually called off my second day and lied about being in a car accident and unable to come to work. The real story was I was scared as hell after day one with a room full of needy second graders. They were crying. They were pulling on me. They couldn't handle the teacher transition as their previous teacher went on maternity leave and would not return. I was the total opposite of what they were used to. I was a black male with authoritarian approaches to managing a classroom versus their former teacher who was a white female with more of an inclusive approach to managing a classroom.

I would teach second grade for one year before proposing to my principal a unique way as it related to teaching third grade the following school year. This was not an ordinary third grade classroom but a third grade all-male classroom. My principal believed in the potential of black males and these particular black males had an elderly teacher with health problems that hampered her teaching and their overall learning. The assignment turned out to be a career changing and saving experience. The following is narrative from this experience that was written in 2001, over seventeen years before I began writing this book:

Educating 3rd Grade Males: A Look Back on the 2000-01 School Year

There were numerous key elements that contributed to our successful school year. I will attempt to state and elaborate on them all. First, the number one key element was the Lord. Without divine intervention, we all would have killed each other from September to June. Second, the element that was most integral was my principal, Dr. William Harris. He allowed me to teach and just be myself. When I proposed the idea of having an all-male class, he said, "You know what, I was thinking the same thing and those boys can really benefit from you." From that point I started looking forward to the next school year (without losing focus on the current school year goals). I had already produced two of the top third grade classrooms my previous two years of teaching. I needed more action, more of a challenge, and this opportunity would prove to be just what I was looking for.

As time passed, the school year ended and many people had heard that I was going to have all males the upcoming school year. Many teachers questioned my sanity and immediately started on how "bad" these boys I was about to inherit were. I heard their comments which went in one ear and out the other. One thing I don't do year after year is prejudge my students. On the first day of school all my students are just that, students. I don't have "Good Students." I don't have "Bad Students." I have academically able persons who are expected to perform on my standards as well as the Chicago Public Schools and State of Illinois standards. When teachers comment in a negative way about my students, out of respect, I hear them but knowing the potential of children, their comments mean nothing. This goes on throughout the entire school year. Students do what they are allowed. Students want and need guidance. I can honestly say I guided my students, all twenty-three of them, every day I was present.

Since I knew I would have all males I decorated my room accordingly. I displayed football posters, basketball posters and posters of hot wheel cars. I used bright-colored instructional posters (comparing books, alphabets, manuscripts, vowel and the scientific method). I used colors mostly related to males such as blue, orange, green and occasionally yellow. There was a key message on each wall which I referred to throughout the school year. On the east wall was poster of a tiger that said, "Perseverance." On the first day of school we looked up the word and I reminded them numerous times to persevere. On the south wall was the message "You Never Know What You Can Do Until You Try." On the west wall, "I Might Fall but I'll Always Get Up." On the north wall was a Michael Jordan poster which simply stated "Reach High!"

We discussed the significance of all these messages and posters the first day of school. This discussion was on-going throughout the school year.

On the first day of school, I proceeded to bring my students into the building from the playground. Many were mistaken when they thought the first day of school was not serious and that it was not business as usual. I had already prepared the daily morning activities: Daily Oral Language: two sentences, bell work and word problem of the day. I had the expected heading on the board and as the students entered the classroom I called their attention to it and told them to get to work. While the students were completing the morning exercises (despite many being visibly upset) I took attendance. At 9:30 a.m. we went over the morning work as a class. This became our morning routine. My students knew what to expect from me and what I expected from them from day one.

After reviewing the morning activities I collected the papers for further skimming. I then proceeded to go over the classroom/ school rules and regulations as well as further expectations for the school year. I allowed my students to have input in setting the classroom rules and corrective actions criteria. After thoroughly going over the rules and expectations, we proceeded to the corridor to discuss proper hallway behavior including the appropriate way to stand in line. I also discussed the corrective actions for not following these rules and expectations. The first week was primarily discussing rules and expectations and allowing them time to adapt.

Also, on the first day of school, I showed the movie *"Rocky IV."* It's a boxing movie starring Sylvester Stallone. This movie supplemented one of my many themes aligned to "change" and expressed that if anyone had any, he would have to change to avoid having a miserable school year. I expressed to my students that many of them will have to change to make it through the school year. I told them their slates are wiped clean and all I ask of them is honest effort. I discussed "bad habits" with them. The first day of school, which is the most important day, went off well, for me.

Throughout the school year, I constantly had to keep my students motivated and interested in the overall concept of important schooling. I started off the year by giving them an abundance of second grade work. This approach was successful. The students gained much needed confidence. The approach acted as a cushion for entering third grade, especially since I didn't know what level each student was on. I wanted to ensure my students didn't just "hit the wall" and lose interest. The second ten weeks of academic instruction showed a decline in grades because third grade material was being introduced and my students had to adjust. One approach that kept them motivated and interested was my implementation of the TGFL, Third Grade Football League. A detailed description of the TGFL is included.

The TGFL consisted of five cooperative teams. Teams consisted of four or five players and there were students designated as reserves who were eligible to play on any team, particularly when someone was not prepared or absent. How were the teams selected? One day we received permission to go outside on the school playground. I had students race each other until we were down to only five students. Those five students each picked one player as their top pick. I pulled another player's name from a container which was the second pick. Finally, the captain (top runner/ racer) picked the final teammate to complete the four player team. Students put forth more effort because there were corrective actions, usually related to their participation in the TGFL, if they didn't complete classroom assignments, homework assignments or behaved inappropriately.

We published weekly TGFL reports that showcased students' academic and athletic talents. The activity was also new and exciting that not only kept my students' attention, but many others around the school as well.

My "Learn through Fun" approach was also reinforced by the various field trips I scheduled for my class throughout the school year. We went on a field trip every month, except for March and April due to I.T.B.S (Iowa Test of Basic Skills) preparation. They weren't just trips just to leave the school building; these were enlightening trips that promoted thinking and reflection. We went to view Toy Story on Ice at the United Center. We saw both high school football and basketball championship games at Soldiers Field and the United Center. Other trips were Lincoln Park Zoo, Drury Lane, Comiskey Park, Navy Pier, the Chicago Theatre and the Rock and Roll McDonald's in downtown Chicago. Of all the trips I think my students enjoyed our trip to Meigs Field the most. On this trip, students learned about aviation, met members of the Tuskegee Airmen and flew around scenic Chicago land. The only thing that was a downfall, not only on this field trip but during the school year, was the lack of parental involvement. I often had to seek assistance from other third grade parents and teachers to have the minimum number of chaperones.

In preparation for the ISAT (Illinois State Assessment Test) and I.T.B.S. (Iowa Test of Basic Skills) we simply dissected the ISAT Coach and Test Best booklets. We covered each unit thoroughly. We would complete the practice items independently, my students would exchange papers at their tables and grade each other's work and reflect on errors and/ or mistakes. After each unit, I would administer the appropriate unit test, grade them myself, return them to students, and then we would dissect various strategies and areas of concern. I really liked the testing schedule of the Chicago Public Schools system that year because as soon as we finished the ISAT in March we moved right into the I.T.B.S. in May. Test subjects and items were still fresh in their minds and I strongly feel this aided them on the I.T.B.S. Since many concepts on the ISAT test are relevant to the concepts on the I.T.B.S we used the ISAT Coach

Preparation booklets along with the Test Best booklets to prepare for the test.

One thing I didn't do with this male group that I did with my previous third grade classes was constantly inform them if they didn't pass the I.T.B.S they would be retained. I used a more relevant approach with this group. Every month, through June, I let them know, through role-playing, lecture and/ or classroom discussion, that the world can function without them and that it was up to them and only them to decide if they would succeed or fail.

Students pretty much know what the I.T.B.S. represents now so my students knew that if you make the score, you pass on to the fourth grade, if you don't make the score, you go to summer school for another try. We were supposed to start that Monday, but testing was cancelled until Tuesday. This gave students more time for nervousness to set in, but I took it in stride and saw it as more review time. That Monday, we reviewed reading skills and strategies in the morning and played football all afternoon. I began each day by supplying the students with an energy boost of graham crackers and orange juice. They completed the reading sections that Tuesday and all five math sections that Wednesday. My students showed fatigue both days, especially Wednesday. After the test Wednesday, we celebrated with soda and chips, it was finally over, at least that's what we thought!

Let me go into the profile of my class so that you can feel the full impact of what I'm about to tell you. My class consisted of twenty-two African-American and one Hispanic male. All but two qualified for free lunch. Of the twenty-three, twenty were below grade level (2.8) in reading at the start of the school year; eighteen were below grade level in math at the start of the school year; seventeen were below grade level in both reading and math; twelve were behind more than one year in reading; eight were behind more than one year in math; and six were behind more than one year in both reading and math. Also, four of my students had kindergarten reading scores and two were retained third graders from the previous school year. This was my class according to the test scores. This data was a result of the 1999-2000 I.T.B.S. scores. What the test scores did not show was the heart and character that these twenty-three young men had.

All year long people questioned the existence of my class. Why would you want all those "bad" boys? What's your purpose? Is the concept of all boys working? These were just a few of the many questions I had to answer all year long. We were about to lay them all to rest and finally shut up the naysayers. The interesting curriculum kept them motivated and excited about school. The integration of the football league played a great role in keeping my students motivated. The discipline forced many of my students to change for the better. The discipline played an important part in their testing. All year long, I gave my students their unit tests in the same manner as I gave the I.T.B.S. I thoroughly read the directions. I asked if everyone understood and were there any questions. I allowed no communication during testing except to raise your hand and I'll help. They knew that if you finish early, read a book or sit quietly, make no noise. Since this was along the same procedure as the I.T.B.S when the test came around my students were familiar and ready to perform. The discipline kept the class focused with no distractions so everyone could do their best.

Did the strategies work? Well, in this decade where test scores say a lot, you judge for yourself. All but two of my students were promoted in June, meaning twenty-one out of twenty-three of my students achieved or scored beyond the minimum promotion score in reading and math which was 3.0. Of the twenty-three, four gained one or more years in reading; six gained two or more years in reading; seven gained three or more years in reading; and one showed a reading growth of four or more years. In math, three gained one or more years; twelve gained two or more years; and five showed a math growth of three or more years. My class averaged two years growth in both reading and math. The year had been a success regardless of what the I.T.B.S. scores were showing, they just added "icing on the cake." The pressure was over, time to relax, or was it?

Keep in mind that we were in the month of May; school is scheduled to end in early June. As the weeks went by I steadily feel uneased about something, but what? Finally, after about three weeks the test scores come back and the staff is informed on numerous occasions not to disclose the scores to students or parents. I'm excited because I see how my students performed, they did exceptionally well but the scores are not official, they're the preliminary scores.

I remember it just like it was yesterday, it was Friday, May 18, 2001. My principal called into my room over the intercom. He said that he wanted to talk to me and that he was coming up. This couldn't have come at a worse time considering I was preparing for our community walk trip around the neighborhood. I was also weary because my principal was coming to me when he could have easily called me down to his office so I knew it was important. Simply put, I was nervous, apprehensive, all that and more. I had to drop two of my students off in another classroom before we left on our trip so I met my principal downstairs. In route, I met Mr. Harris and he didn't hesitate. He said, "Dase, we (Lawrence School) have been selected for this year's annual audit and your class along with one of my eighth grade classes will have to retest." As you can probably imagine, my heart dropped and almost instantly, my excitement turned into anger and resentment. I almost broke down in tears but Mr. Harris immediately sensed my anger and gave me a swift but stern lecture. He informed me that this was life and that if I plan on becoming an administrator that I shouldn't take situations such as this personal. Yes, my integrity, the school's integrity (as Chicago Public Schools puts it) was in question. We had three days to prepare for the retest and just like Mr. Harris stated "You get those boys motivated and you all show them that this wasn't a fluke, you did it once and I have all confidence that you can do it again." That's one great thing about Mr. Harris; he believes in your abilities and exerts the best from you at all times. I mentioned earlier that I needed more action, more of a challenge; well the ultimate challenge was before me. I had to get my students motivated and ready to perform their best a second time!

I thought about the situation at hand all weekend. I had nightmares about letting my students down. I was determined that no one or nothing was going to blemish this wonderful school year. What do I tell my students? I talked it over with my wife. I talked it over with Mr. Davis, our assistant principal. Finally, that following Monday I passed out the ISAT Coach and Test Best booklets. My students had that look of "what the hell is going on?" I simply said, "Remember when I told you that no one cares if you succeed or fail, that it's up to you? Well seems that our scores are in question and we have to retest this coming Thursday." Many of my students were confused. Many of my students took the news well. I told them that some of them performed poorly so this would give them another opportunity. I didn't reveal who would have passed or failed because I didn't want a letdown the second time around. I told them that basically the first test scores were "garbage" and if they want to be promoted the retest is the one that counts. I told them "that's life, we have to do this." We prepared Monday, Tuesday and Wednesday. We took the reading retest Thursday and the math retest Friday.

The retest didn't go as smoothly as the previous I.T.B.S testing sessions. One reason was because the Board of Education, region 6, or whoever sent the tester, sent a female. Now this wouldn't disrupt many classrooms but for ours a little. Considering there had only been one female to stay over thirty minutes in one setting all year long. That was our proctor and my close friend, Ms. Shea, the physical education teacher. This could have been a distraction because she would be the primary tester, not me. Besides being a female she was also Caucasian. Now this was one aspect that we hadn't encountered all year long. When I first saw her I simply laughed. It was getting to the point where that's all I could do is laugh, stay upbeat for my students and support them. The retesting went better than expected; having a Caucasian, female tester didn't seem to affect my students at all. What did start to show was their frustration and fatigue from the very first day of retesting. I was not the tester but I was a thorough proctor, keeping their heads up, making sure they filled in their answers completely and most important making sure they didn't waste time. I can remember on the first day of retest, there was an assembly for grades K-4 and the announcement was made over the intercom system. Don't ask me why or how but many of my students thought they were attending and literally stopped testing and closed their test booklets. I almost blew a gasket, I was so upset. I was upset at the announcer for disrupting our testing session and I was upset at many of my student for once again not using "common sense." During each break which was every twenty minutes I gave each student a giant now-or-later to chew. This provided them with sugar to keep them alert for the duration of the retests.

Thursday and Friday passed, the retests were over. One thing I can say is that if we have to ever retest again I wouldn't mind having the woman we had this go round. She was friendly and actually aided in making my students and I feel comfortable. That Friday, we said "goodbye" to the tester and proceeded to go on our last field trip of the school year, to McDonald's for what we (my third grade colleagues and I) called our third grade luncheon. The field trip turned out great considering once again, I didn't have one parent from my room to attend. Now my students and I would begin our second waiting period to see if we upheld our integrity or diminished it a tad bit.

We would have a four-day weekend (Memorial Day weekend) and a maximum of nine school days to wait to hear about our fate. I just knew the scores would come back that following week but they didn't. We were actually the only class in the school who hadn't received confirmation on our scores. Even the eighth graders who retested went on with their regularly scheduled activities despite not hearing about their retest scores. When I heard about that I basically said, "The hell with it." I was tired of waiting. My students were tired of waiting. Parents were tired of waiting. I guess Mr. Harris was tired of waiting as well because the following week (the last week of school) he released the preliminary scores. Everybody was excited, many were amazed. Since we hadn't heard anything about the retest the big question was "are these scores going to stand?" My big answer was "I don't know."

The third grade teachers (my colleagues and I) had planned an end of the year pizza party to celebrate a wonderful school year. The last day of school comes and we're still wondering should we celebrate or cry? The previous day I had already talked to my students about not hearing anything about the retest scores. I told them that if that bell rings on Friday at 2:30 p.m. and we still haven't heard anything that the preliminary scores would stand and to have a wonderful summer. On Friday, we just waited around finishing up our time capsule project. Every student wrote about the school year, what they liked, what they didn't like and we enclosed these writings and other memorable items into our plastic "time capsule." The plan was to open when this class enters eighth grade, towards graduation. At approximately 10:00 a.m., Mr. Harris walks through the door. He's "G-ed up" in his gray suit, stepping proudly. My heart starts jumping because I know what he had in his hands, the retest results. My heart was beating so fast I thought I was going to faint. All I remember is Mr. Harris saying "they did better than before. See I told you, when you believe in yourself and you have faith, truth will prevail." The waiting was over, we had conquered. Mr. Harris informed my students of the good news; the room was filled with smiles. He also informed my two colleagues of the good news and they came over giving everyone hugs and kisses. It was truly wonderful and finally we could celebrate. I was so excited that I told everyone to stop working and that what we had already would go into the time capsule. For the rest of the day we celebrated. We had our pizza party, we watched movies, we ate candy and of course, we played football!

Other Notable Events: A Look Back on the 2000-01 School Year

As I stated, there was very little parental involvement throughout the school year. Out of the few who did take out time to come see about their son's progress regularly it was one who stood out and who I would say "had my back." This one parent expressed to me during the first report card pick up in November of 2000 that many parents who knew their child was in an all-male classroom were upset. This parent told me that they were upset because they weren't informed of the situation. They were upset because they felt their child was being labeled or discriminated against because of his behavior. When this parent told me these things I was initially surprised. I was surprised because on my syllabus of rules, regulations and expectations I clearly stated that it was an all-male classroom. Many parents returned their portion where I requested a signature of acknowledgement. Some parents didn't return it at all. This let me know that most of my parents don't read what's sent home regularly.

The issue of being labeled or discriminated against simply told me what I already knew, that parents are aware of their child's behavior or lack of behavior and try to put up a smoke screen when you tell them their child misbehaves. Coming from only one parent and here it is two months into the school year also let me know that these parents were not going to be vocal about their concerns. This is part of the reason I began not valuing homework as much as I did in the past. Don't get me wrong, homework is a very important aspect of a child's education and development but if a child has to literally force someone who loves them to help them then how much blame can you lay on the student. Some of the blame, more than likely, most of the blame can be put on the student, but parents play an important role in discipline and habits and must do their part.

Another notable event worth mentioning was when one of my students accused me of discriminating against him. Although he was the only Hispanic in my room he didn't accuse me of racial discrimination. He simply felt that I singled him out and "picked on him" all the time. As anyone can imagine, I was deeply disturbed about this issue. He had problems with my discipline tactics. He had problems with other students picking on him. All this resulting in me singling him out. One day while being redirected for excessive talking he told me "his rights." He said he hated me. He said he wished I was dead. He went on and on about how I was the worst person on the face of this earth. Finally, the situation between us got so bad that he had to be transferred to another classroom. Little did he and his mother know that he was being transferred into another classroom where the teacher is as stern as me if not more and that she would pick up the phone in a minute to call about any misbehavior. I'm a stern man and require discipline but one thing I don't do much of and that is call about misbehavior. I handle it all within my four walls.

I had seen his mother for report card pick up and scheduled a meeting with my principal about the discrimination accusations. When he was transferred, I saw her at least three times a week, inside the building. She was a concerned parent but she didn't want to be at the school that much especially for something negative. After about four weeks, his mother requested that he transfer back into my classroom. My principal left the decision solely up to me with a little advice about how he needs to be with me again. I thought about it for about a week. His mother, my principal and I had another conference. We all met with the social worker for another conference. I decided to allow him to return to my classroom under two conditions. One condition was that he and his mother sign a contract acknowledging my expectations. The other condition was him stating that he wanted to return to my classroom. Initially he stated that he did not want to return to my classroom. His mother requested that I give him a little more time to think about it. About two days later he stated he wanted to return. He returned for the final fifteen weeks of the school year. I figured his mother convinced him to say he wanted to return. It was evident because numerous times after he returned he would state "I hate this class, I wish my mother would have never made me come back." Bottom line, he wanted to have his way and he couldn't get it with me so he made up some lies at an attempt to make me look bad and get him out of my class. I say lies because about a month after the accusations were brought forward he admitted he had made it all up and his mother brought it to my principal's and my attention. This was another involved parent and I credit her support because without it the situation could have been much worse. As I knew from the first week of school, he was one of my brightest students; he just did not ever apply himself fully. Despite all the mobility, he scored the highest in reading on the I.T.B.S. and made the most progress/ growth in reading on the I.T.B.S. He's one of those students who you know has all the potential in the world but just doesn't do this best, one of those students who keep you going that extra mile.

I had many students that would keep you going but one other that stood out was the one I call the "Knowledgeable Street Thug." This student was street-smart and school smart. The teachers who had him previously labeled him a "troublemaker "and a "gang banger." He and I battled all year long. If it wasn't for his kind grandmother I probably would have been going to court for doing something to this kid. My motto was "you come to school to learn, leave all that other nonsense outside." People, teachers would always tell me they saw him on the street doing this or doing that. Whether he did this or that when he came to school he applied himself more than most. He had his bad days but I didn't mind them so much because he would try. His grandfather said he needed a strong presence and to "stay on his butt." I did just that, stayed on him to produce positive results with his academics and character. He turned out to be one of the most responsible young men in my classroom. He was a good listener and he wanted to excel. He made the honor roll for the first time and was one of my first students to join my 2001 golf team. He passed the I.T.B.S. with little difficulty. When his grandmother received the scores in the mail she called and said thank you and that they were proud of him. I told her that they should be because he passed primarily because he listened. School is not everything which is evident with this young man because the street has given him valuable knowledge as well.

Another notable event was the unveiling of our TGFL (Third Grade Football League) display. I set it up directly across from the main office. It was revealed on report card pick-up day for the third marking period. I'm not trying to brag but it was the best display all year. I displayed our weekly reports, note sheets, statistics, pictures and most important, trophies. The display read: Third Grade Football League: Who Said Learning Isn't Fun? The students took pride in the display. They felt wonderful seeing their names on the trophies and various pictures taken. I even had every student sign the official TGFL football and displayed it with their signatures. The display stayed untouched until the fourth and last marking period when they would receive their trophies at the school's annual academic awards ceremony. I received many kind words about the display. It was one of my best displays since coming to Lawrence School.

Another notable event and the last to be mentioned is the annual Robert H. Lawrence Awards Ceremony. For many students this would be their only opportunity to be in the spotlight. As many will tell you I took full advantage of the spotlight. Every one of my students received an award, not just any award, but an award they deserved. Everyone received a physical education pin for participating in the TGFL. Many received academic awards for reading, math, science, social sciences and writing. I also gave the I.T.B.S. motivation awards away. Before the I.T.B.S. I displayed four trophies that could be won. The two bigger trophies would go to the student or students that scored the highest in reading and math on the I.T.B.S. The two smaller trophies would go to the student or students that made the most progress in reading and math. One of my students made the most progress in reading. One of my students scored the highest in math. I also gave out the TGFL trophies. I gave out a most valuable player trophy, a player of the year trophy, an offensive player of the year trophy, a defensive player of the year trophy, a super bowl most valuable player trophy and each member of the super bowl winning team, the Quinton Jets, received individual super bowl trophies. One student received four trophies, four academic certificates and one pin. The audience was amazed. Some thought we were trying to show off but we weren't. I gave everyone an award out of love. I loved that group of young men and I loved the school year despite the obstacles.

All Males, Not All Year: A Look Back on the 2000-01 School Year

Being a male who often needs a female, I didn't totally isolate my males from the female population of the school. They often went to the computer lab with one of my other third grade colleagues who had female students in her class. During lunch time they were allowed to interact with the other classes that had female students. My two third grade colleagues, who were females, often came in to talk to them and help with their disciplining. My wife, the first grade teacher, would often come help and have discussions with my males on her break. Although I had an all-male classroom they were very much interactive with the female population of Robert H. Lawrence. Towards the end of the school year I organized a Beta House Tag Football Tournament. Several teams were all-female and they competed against the males. One female team made it to the semifinals. Throughout the school year, we would research and discuss famous females and their accomplishments. I would have discussions with them about my wonderful wife and our two lovely daughters. Even at the awards ceremony, I gave them an example of how you show appreciation. I gave my wife a trophy that read "Wife of the Year." I often instructed them to always show appreciation before it's too late to do so. Most important, I told them to never disrespect a female and always appreciate them because without them there would be no us. They listened and all year long we had no problems except for the substitute teacher but hey, you can't win them all!

Special Thanks to:

The Lord

William Harris, My Principal

Charles Davis, My Assistant Principal

Irene Dase, My Wife

Jakia Dase, My Daughter

Asia McDonald, My Daughter

James Hayes, My Father

Annie Bryant, My Mother

James Bryant, My Step Father

Clarence Clair, My Best Friend

Denise Sydney, My Colleague

Joyce Berry, My Colleague

My "Twenty-Three Crew" – My Students

CHAPTER 6

Footprints, You Don't Stand Alone

Again, teaching an all-male classroom was a career changing and saving experience. The words in this book do not do justice for the overall experience and joy teaching those boys brought to my life. There are some success stories that come from that classroom such as Daniel Abankwa, Gates Millennium Scholarship recipient; and there are some tragic stories that come from that classroom such as the student serving time for multiple attempted murders. I have kept in contact with many of my young men. And to think, I almost decided to stay at Kohn School to start my teaching career. What a difference one decision can make. I went on to become a successful teacher, get hired by my principal as an assistant principal when he moved on and being mentored into the principalship by the same man while Kohn School would decline in student achievement and enrollment, and eventually close. That one decision saved my career. It came with guidance from another male mentor, my supervising teacher at Kohn School, Dr. William Johnson. Dr.

Johnson convinced me to leave Kohn School for Lawrence School after my student teaching year at Kohn. He has remained my mentor and supporter throughout my career with Chicago Public Schools.

Being a Chicago Public Schools teacher was definitely full of ups and downs but the ups far outweigh the downs. I am a black male in a predominately female driven profession. We were a tight knit group of professionals at Lawrence that worked hard and played hard. William Harris who became Dr. William Harris believed in having a work-life balance. We would do lesson plans together and attend parties together. Everyone was interested in the new young teacher. I became close with several of the teachers who provided me guidance in and outside the classroom. One of the employees eventually became a teacher and worked for me when I was a principal. She had my back since day one. Every day was a test of loyalty for her because she did not ever disclose how close our relationship was and still is.

I developed life-long relationships at Lawrence. Several of us still support each other to this day and are close friends that encourage each other's professional and personal growth. When I receive recognition, several of them are front row cheering me on, and I have done the same for them. We've attended family events and often communicate whether for a short or long time to keep in touch. Lawrence School was my first family with Chicago Public Schools. Lawrence School allowed me the opportunity to flourish and grow. Many of them take pride in my success because they know they were and still are a part of my upbringing as it relates to moving through the ranks of Chicago Public Schools.

It was summer of 2002 and I had just returned from one of the best trips I have ever taken with my best friend Clarence. We took a week trip to New York and Florida. When I say "we kicked it" that would be an understatement. It was a non-stop experience except for the occasional naps we called sleep at the time. One of the days in Orlando we just decided we wanted to go see South Beach, Miami. The only thing was it was two and a half hours away and we had a scheduled party to attend at the Orlando BET Night Club that night. We looked at each other and said @#$% it, let's go. We drove to South Beach, Miami, viewed the area for a while and discovered one of the nude beaches. Let's just say the nude beach was over-rated.

On our way back to Orlando that evening, we literally did not go under 100 miles per hour . We made it back to Orlando in time to attend the party. The next day, our final day in Orlando, Clarence wanted some seafood, his favorite food, so we went to Red Lobster. I remember the waitress asking us did we want anything to drink as in alcohol and both of us were like "hell no." Our bodies had begun to shut down from all the drinking and experimenting. We literally drank at least one twelve pack of beer daily on that trip. It would be one of many exciting trips me and Clarence would enjoy together.

Getting back on my career track, I remember getting a call from Coach Smith (rest in peace) who had just acquired the security position at Julian High School. I remember him saying congratulations. I asked for what? He said on being our new assistant principal. He said Dr. Harris announced it in the staff meeting today. Now mind you, I was at home enjoying the rest of my summer vacation. I immediately called Dr. Harris after getting off the phone with Coach Smith and asked him if there was something he wanted to share with me? He laughed and said "I told you you were coming with me." This man had hired me as his assistant principal of Percy L. Julian High School, my alma mater, without telling me. I interviewed for the position but he had not given me a call back but hey, I was nervous as hell but excited on my journey. Once again, William Harris would take a chance on me as one of the youngest assistant principals in Chicago Public Schools at the time. I was 27 years old. News traveled fast around the school district and the city of Chicago about my new assignment. Many were excited for me and many were like "how the hell did he get that position?" You know, haters. Dr. Harris was a man who was true to his words and philosophy of giving back and helping young black males become the next leaders within the school district. The haters were everywhere. I remember being at the check-out counter in the grocery store when I saw my girl Delisa, my former love, and she told me you know people hating on you, they are wondering how you got the position. I told her that's cool, if they want to know tell them to ask me face to face.

Needless to say, the cowards did not surface in my face and I went on to have a successful four-year tenure as assistant principal at Julian High School. It felt strange being in a higher position than and supervising teachers who'd given me grades in high school, but as I stated earlier, they took pride in my success because they literally were a part of my success story. Many people tried to take advantage of me being new to administration and my overall youth, including staff and students. I remember the security team and I would always have conflict over them not checking identification cards and allowing students that did not belong in the lunchroom. It became so predictable that one day I finalized disciplinary papers to issue to them because I knew they were going to disobey my directive and allow students that did not belong in the lunchroom at the time to enter. I even called my buddy, my mentor, my administrative coach, Mr. Reynolds over to my office to observe my leadership actions. I let the lunchroom fill up and went in and randomly checked students identification cards. Sure enough, there were numerous students that did not belong in the lunchroom. I did not tell the students to leave or cause a scene. I called each security officer to my office one at a time, presented them with their disciplinary papers, they signed and exited my office. Both were pissed but the word spread quickly throughout the staff and school that I was not playing games with them and slowly but surely the respect and productivity increased. Just like with the students, unfortunately, sometimes you have to make an example of one, two or some for everyone else to fall in line and take you seriously.

This was not limited to staff. I had to make an example of a student as well. My first day on the job as assistant principal, I was standing near the lunchroom entrance and I hear a student right behind me say "who this stripe suit wearing motherfucker?" I turned around slowly and stated, well let me show you who this stripe suit wearing dude is, come on to my office son. Everybody started laughing at him and saying, damn, who is dude referring to me. This hardcore, profanity-laced student followed me to my office and sat down. I extended my hand out to him and said, "Nice meeting you I'm the assistant principal--call me Mr. Dase--and congratulations, you will be my first suspension, what's your parent's number?" As I called his parent and explained the incident and corrective actions that I would be issuing, he sat in my office chair speechless. That was the beginning of my firm but fair approach to leadership. Julian High School was a true battle ground for leadership but it was so rewarding. It was there that I learned to individualize my approach to students. They were hard as hell as a group but almost every one of them showed you a genuine kid side one on one. We dealt with some stone cold gang bangers at Julian and to be honest; those were some of the best kids also.

You name it, we had it at Julian, but the kids still received a solid education and showed out. During my tenure at Julian we were removed off the academic probation list despite all the negative rumors about the school. Dr. Harris once again built a family environment and pride at Julian. We definitely had more good than bad days during that time. It's where I formed some of my lasting professional and personal relationships that are still tight to this day, such as the ones with Renee Sims and Richadine Murry, the other assistant principals at the time. I mentioned Mr. Reynolds, Eddie Reynolds, stone cold old school administrator who taught me a lot about leadership. Mr. Reynolds was the Dean of Students. He lasted a long time. He was Dean of Students when I was a student at Julian between 1989 and 1993. He was so fierce. I once saw him scare a student out of his shoes just from hearing Mr. Reynolds' voice around the corner. I remember a wheelchair student accused him of touching her inappropriately. Now most people nowadays would be worried about that allegation, not Mr. Reynolds. He told the female student, in the presence of her parents that she was lying and to turn around and face him with all those lies. We laugh about that incident to this day.

Mr. Reynolds was a beast. Students did not appreciate him until they left and became adults. He taught real life skills. He had a hard exterior but a soft interior. He would give kids hats and scarves for the holiday and cook for the homeless often. He was a chef in the Army and we benefited often from his culinary skills. We would often gather together after the last lunch period to eat lunch together in his conference room. During his last year with Chicago Public Schools, he was allowed to go to any school of his choice and he came with me at Coles School where I was the principal at the time. I was honored to present him with a retirement plaque upon his retirement. He taught me so much and I was honored for him to retire under my leadership at my school. PRICELESS!

I would remain at Julian for four years until 2007, which was a rough school year for us at Julian High School. It was the year Blair Holt was killed on a Chicago Transit Authority (CTA) bus by another Julian student. I knew both students well and just like he was portrayed, Blair Holt was an excellent student and young man. He had great parents. I still keep in touch with his dad to this day. He has participated in many of my black male mentoring events throughout the years. The young man that killed Blair was troubled but not an evil kid. He would get into a lot of trouble but was approachable and he would listen in a one-on-one setting. It was unfortunate but two lives were lost from that incident.

2007 was also the year Dr. Harris announced his retirement and an immediate power struggle started between two camps that developed over the years at Julian High School. One camp included those in favor of Dr. Harris and his pick to succeed him…which was me. The other camp included those in favor of another former administrator at Julian and his pick to succeed Dr. Harris which was the other assistant principal. The other assistant principal was the main assistant principal of the school. To this day, I don't know the extent of the other assistant principal's involvement in the power struggle but one day I asked to meet privately with him about the overall rumors and atmosphere. I told him point blank, I'm not taking sides and if I was selected to be principal, I would retain him as assistant principal and if he was selected as principal, I would be honored to serve as his assistant principal. I remember him listening and offering no comment which was strange to me, but I had said my piece and was at peace.

Come time to interview for the principalship, he decided to drop out. I heard he felt it was rigged in my favor, but to this day, I don't know why he dropped out. I went through the interview process and made it to the Local School Council (LSC) Forum with two other candidates, one being Dr. Murry, the other assistant principal at Julian at the time. We had already discussed and decided whoever would be principal would keep the other as one of the assistant principals. People did try to give me questions and answers before the forum but I refused to accept because I needed to acquire the principalship on my own merit. I ended up being the finalist for the Julian principal selection, but the LSC decided to offer me an interim principal position instead of a four year contract. This is what many people don't know as I've been questioned for years as to why I left Julian High School. People also didn't know that I was offered a four-year contract at Dunne Elementary School the previous school year but gave up that opportunity after talking to the LSC of Julian because they wanted me to stay at Julian to succeed Dr. Harris.

For the LSC to offer me an interim principal assignment was a slap in the face to me. An interim principal assignment had no contract or security so the minute I didn't do what they wanted, I would be out the door. When they offered me the interim principal assignment, I laughed and told them I would seek a four-year contract elsewhere. This is when tension heated up all over the school because both successors were about to leave the school. This is when Dr. Harris and I fell out with one another and communication became minimal. I felt he controlled the process and the LSC and had a lot to do with the interim principal assignment offer, not to mention he completed the budget for the next school year without any input from me. It included a $90,000.00 salary for himself as a consultant. They basically wanted a puppet, and as the kids say "I ain't going."

I began my search to acquire a principalship, and it wasn't hard at the time. Many schools were looking for a strong black male to lead their school and community. I recall telling one LSC at the principal selection forum that they might want to make a decision soon because there were no guarantees I would be available the next week. In hindsight, that statement was cocky as hell but read what happened. While I was interviewing for principal positions, Julian's LSC was trying to convince me to take the interim principal position. I kept refusing. Staff members were upset because they didn't know the future of the school or of their jobs so it's increased emotions to say the least. The time period was so stressful for me as it related to making a decision that I joined church and asked the Lord to guide me to making the right decision. I joined church that Sunday and the next week, I received a call from a Mrs. Shervia Randall, Coles Elementary School Local School Council (LSC) teacher representative and she stated after asking to speak to me by name "the Lord is telling me you are the next principal of our school." She had called to schedule an interview for me to come before the LSC to interview for the Coles Elementary School principal position. After we talked and scheduled the date and time of the interview, I remember hanging up the phone, looking up and saying, "thank you, Lord" as I sat down and began to cry.

Even though I had not interviewed or stepped foot into Coles School, I knew that is where I would be principal. It felt like a boulder was lifted off my shoulders. I would go on to interview for the principal position at Coles School. I almost was late as I went to the wrong school on the day of the interview. I went to Mann School on Jeffery Street which looks identical to Coles School on Yates Street. Luckily, I left time to arrive early and be told I'm at the wrong school so I could make it to Coles on time for the interview. I would make the final list of candidates to participate in the community forum. To show you how petty people can be, the chairperson of Julian's LSC got word I was one of the finalist for the Coles principal position and he threatened to show up and disclose that I had given up a principal position in the past and that I may be unreliable. As I was answering questions on the stage at the community forum, he actually showed up and sat in the audience. I performed well and articulated my vision for the school. The LSC decided to vote on their choice immediately after the community forum concluded. As everyone in the auditorium is waiting, they come back and announce Jeffery Dase will be our next principal at Coles School. I walk off the stage, people are congratulating me, people are talking to me and the Julian LSC chairperson comes up, gives me a hug and says congratulations.

The following day as I'm back working at Julian (I would not start as principal of Coles until July 1, 2007), the clerk called my office and told me a parent from a school was here to see me. I told her to let him up. It's the parent representative from the school I'd told may want to make a decision soon. He asks me why I didn't choose his school. I told him I did not hear back from them. He was sad because he said I was the selection and he felt I would have been a great role model for the students, especially the black males. We talked awhile and he left but the Lord guided me in the right direction. After enduring more turmoil and bickering, the Harris Administration at Julian High School would end that June in 2007. All four assistant principals including myself would leave to lead other schools. I, Dr. Murry and the other assistant principal would go on to lead elementary schools in the district. We all would lead schools in the districts Network 17 at the time so we would continue to see a lot of each other. Renee Sims would go on to lead a high school in the south suburbs. Dr. Harris would retire. I began the next chapter of my Chicago Public Schools career as the newly-selected principal at Coles Elementary School on the southeast side of Chicago on July 1, 2007.

The next era of my career as principal of Edward Coles Language Academy ... Where do I start? Actually, it starts not at Coles but back at Julian High School during the month of June 2007 when we all departing assistant principals interviewed assistant principal candidates together at Julian High School. We interviewed this young man who we will always remember as a little nervous, so nervous somehow we noticed (or he mentioned) he had on mix-match socks. We laugh about that to this day. We all were very impressed with the young man. I had a little more background about this candidate as I was fortunate enough to see him in action on several occasions prior to his interview. He was a football coach for Julian High School. I was the administrator in charge of the school's sports program so I would often travel with the teams. I remembered we traveled down state for a football game and I was hanging out after the game with the coaches. We were all in front of a bar and grill and another young man walked by with his girlfriend. One of us, might have been me, commented on the girlfriend's physique, nothing disrespectful, but the comment was amongst us. The young man overheard the comment and came back to confront us. This young man that we are interviewing kindly informed the other young man it would be in his best interest to continue walking with his girlfriend. The young man continues to talk and all of a sudden he was hit with two quick slaps. The young man took the slaps like a man and said, "That didn't even hurt." The conversation the rest of the night was about how that young man is going to gain his dignity back after being slapped in front of this girlfriend and then doing absolutely nothing. Now I don't condone violence, but in that case, either I was going to hurt someone or I would have been hurt. I couldn't have just walked away, especially being with my girlfriend. The young man really should have taken the advice and walked off. If he wanted to say something, say it from a distance but not while in the middle of five adult men who are either 6 feet or near 300 pounds. It's a no win situation. As men, sometimes we have to suck in our pride and live to talk about it another day.

The young man who handled the situation politely but quickly is known as El-Roy Estes. He would become my assistant principal. That hire began my era as principal of Coles School. He was one of my best hires of my career. We would establish a partnership and bond that is indescribable and effective as hell. After conducting a needs assessment, I quickly learned most stakeholders were seeking some structure at Coles. They felt their males were out of control so myself and El-Roy were the perfect duo to get this ship back sailing right again. Over the summer we called in all the identified "bad" students, met with them and their parents and informed them we didn't care about their past, we were wiping the slate clean and they would have a fair opportunity to be great students. The alternative would be the swift and firm corrective actions that would follow if you disrupted the process we are trying to establish at Coles. All were receptive and thankful. We spent the summer preparing for opening our school in September 2007.

The opening day of school with the new dynamic duo of Dase and Estes was postponed for several days as the vegan Estes decided to do a detox the weekend before opening day and ended up in the hospital so I was solo on opening day as principal. Opening day was filled with excitement including parents coming in demanding their children be placed in certain classrooms and with certain students and teachers. I professionally addressed all inquiries and provided rationales for decision. The day was rough, but remember I came from Julian High School. I was more than prepared. I always said it was easier coming from high school to elementary school than it would have been going up to a high school from an elementary school to lead as principal. We were set up in small school settings at Julian. I had 750 students in my Beta House wing so I was prepared for Coles 600 students and parents.

Once El-Roy returned, he would be charged with Middle School grades while I focused on the primary grades and establishing our school's foundation. We shared the intermediate grades. Leaders of elementary schools must ensure they have a solid early childhood and primary structure or you will constantly be applying a "Band-Aid" and filling temporary gaps instead of having pre-kindergarten through eighth grade excellence. I made sure my best teachers were in my primary grades first and held everybody else accountable for maintaining and increasing that learning as my students moved through the grades at Coles. Our first year, specifically our first four months at Coles, we were visible and observed practices that were going on in the classrooms so we could assess whether to adjust, enhance or remove. I recall walking on the second floor one day and a teacher said, "Wow, the principal is on the second floor, that's a change." That told me right there the previous principal was not visible enough. During entrance and dismissal, El-Roy and I made sure we were present and walking the grounds until the last student entered the building or went home for the day. The majority of our administration meetings took place outside on school grounds either in the morning or dismissal. That was also the time we established relationships with our community. They appreciated the presence and always knew they could find us before or after school without an appointment.

The next key to the puzzle was the hiring of a school counselor in which we had a vacancy. We involved teachers and the Local School Council (LSC) in most hires. We went through a lengthy process because this was a critically important position. I wanted my counselor to handle student development, which included social and emotional development and high school preparation, so we had to get this one right the first time. We ended up selecting Valerie Galmore as our counselor that would help us propel into greatness. Although she is crazy as hell, she proved to be the right choice and best for our kids. She was disorganized and did things at the drop of a hat, but one thing she had was a huge heart. She wanted kids to experience everything life could offer and if life wasn't offering it then she felt it was our obligation to provide the experience for them. Although Ms. Glamore was a critical hire, the person who helped us navigate the past and clear any current hurdles was a fine, old school diva named Ms. Pamela Foster. Ms. Foster was the glue in our dynamic three headed administration team. She had served at Coles for over 30 years and took us in as her own. Even though we were technically the bosses, she was the true boss.

We inherited some dynamic veteran staff members. People today don't want to higher veterans because they label them as on the downside of their career but the veterans were the ones that helped us greatly in establishing solid systems and structures at Coles. They would implement at a higher rate than the younger teachers and serve as models throughout the school building. The veteran teachers were our biggest cheerleaders. They saw the potential and possibilities and wanted to be a part of the change at Coles. Their buy-in bought us time and respect. Although not a veteran but with drive out of this world was our math coach, Eboni McDonald. Not only was she dynamic at developing our teachers' pedagogy but she would take an idea and develop it to unimaginable realms. Student incentive ideas, motivational ideas, games, whatever, she would develop and implement masterpieces that made us look like geniuses. Our biggest and most exciting event of the school year was an idea from Eboni McDonald, the Coles B.E.T Awards Event.

BET was the acronym we used for Boosting Educational Talents and it was an event in which staff would honor students for their outstanding performance the previous school year and served as motivation for the current school year. Staff would dress up and do cameo appearances as famous stars. In between performances, we would present students with awards in different categories such as high achievement on a standardized assessment to honor roll for all quarters of the school year. Eboni eventually left Coles and became an assistant principal at another Chicago Public School and Ms. Galmore became the lead of this event. By the time I left Coles as principal this event was the most attended of any Coles community event. It was a standing room only event. It went from staff and students to staff, students, community, parents and district officials attending. The Chief Education Officer at the time and current Chief Executive Officer of Chicago Public Schools, Dr. Janice Jackson attended the last year I was principal at Coles.

So much happened during my tenure at Coles it is not possible to capture in one chapter or part of a chapter. My tenure at Coles is a book itself. We completed a true rags-to-riches story as we propelled one of the lowest performing schools into one of the highest performing schools in the district. I often would refer to us as functioning crack heads because on paper we looked dynamic but there was a lot to deal with even when we were on top as a Level 1+ school. As a Level 3 school, low-performing school and newly assigned principal, I had to handle the effects of change. Many people did not want change despite the school's performance. They would post lies in the community newspaper about this young, new principal that wanted to fire all the veteran staff members.

There were staff members who knew other staff members were physically and psychologically hurting students but turned a blind eye until one staff member's own kids endured the mistreatment. It was then when my actions to remove bad seeds became justifiable. I was blamed for damn near everything, even a teacher's death. I always say, with results get you respect, well positive results get you respect. We increased student achievement and decreased student discipline every year under my tenure as Coles principal. It was hard work but as the famous quote says "anything worth having is worth the blood, sweat and tears." We eventually moved from negative interactions to positive highlights throughout the years. As the recognition started coming and behaviors started to change we grew together as a tight-knit family.

Even then there were some bumps in the road, for example, one year I was accused of being a racist against, get this, my own people, black folks. I was called downtown to interview with the district investigators about the allegations because the controversy made the internet and the local news. This followed a poorly-planned staff meeting about race and how teachers' race matters with preparation and expectations to our black kids. I offended black staff members and after a series of intentional discussion sessions, I understood their view and apologized for any unintentional offense I caused. Luckily, at that time, the school was progressing in the positive so many understood my error and forgave me as we moved on as a staff. We had quarterly scheduled outings whether at a staff member's house or at a venue. These events really built our bond as a staff. Everyone couldn't come to each event but throughout the school year most would make it to at least one event. One of the highlights was when we took a staff skiing retreat in Lake Geneva, Wisconsin. I had to leave early that year because I was attending the All-Star Weekend events but it really was a bonding experience for the staff. I would often make an appearance and leave early so the staff could enjoy each other without Big Brother Administration in the room. Surprisingly, more often than not, staff wanted us to stay and engage in the partying with them. No celebration ever got out of hand except for the 2015 end of the year party which included El-Roy and I bumping heads but we had our moment, talked to each other the day after and eventually moved on. That was the beauty about Coles, there was a lot, and I mean a lot of disputes and conflict but we sucked up our personal feelings for the professional benefit of the whole, the team, Coles School. My goal was always to get the school removed from the probation list, not making Level 1 or Level 1+. I knew with strong academic progress those other accolades would be a byproduct of success. I remember getting the preliminary results in October of 2012 that we were Level 1 and off probation. I told no one except El-Roy and planned a community meeting on the same day the district would officially announce the school performance results. There was a representative who spoke on the school progress from each stakeholder group from staff, students, community, and parents. When I gave the closing remarks, I asked the students in the audience to stand. I proceeded to tell them that when they wake up in the morning to look in the mirror and smile and tell yourself I now attend one of the top schools in Chicago Public Schools that is off probation and a Level 1 school in good standing. The auditorium erupted in celebration from all stakeholders. There were teachers, students and parents crying. I remember one of the community parents who son was just killed that year, but continued to support our efforts come up to me and say "you did it" as he hugged me. For individuals who were there since day one in 2007, they knew what it took to reach that point and you could hear a huge exhale over the auditorium. The following day I posted prepared signs in the grass around the school that read "COLES SCHOOL, LEVEL 1, GOOD STANDING SCHOOL, OFF PROBATION, GREAT STUDENTS, GREAT STAFF, GREAT PARENTS"

We were all excited. It was a true story of perseverance and grit paying off. We would go on to maintain and increase our school status to the highest at Level 1+ until I was called to the next journey of my career path with Chicago Public Schools. I left a legacy and empire at Coles School. From the BET awards event, to Winter Ball, to our Haunted House on Halloween, to our annual overnight male mentoring event Brotherhood, Books and Ballin, to the Puerto Rico, San Francisco, Washington, D.C. and New York student trips, to single gender classrooms, to increasing student performance and parent participation, Coles School from 2007 to 2016 was a model for school change and school reform. We figured it out midway through the journey when we, all the adults were grinding to improve student achievement. Once we tapped into the students' mindset and instilled the importance of them performing well, we took off as it related to overall school achievement growth and attainment. The next year after we started talking to students and holding student goal setting sessions we moved up to non-probation level school. We had to maintain or increase to officially be removed and we did it. It's hard for me to use "I" when talking about Coles

School's success because it was truly a team effort. For example, I wanted to implement single-gender classrooms at Coles and we implemented single gender classrooms as well as looping with your students structures. The experiment worked so well, teachers began to have conflict over who would teach the students the next school year because they had to maintain or increase the high academic students' performance.

I remember Ms. Loretha Brown taking on the challenge of a high performing all-male classroom. Even though I had a high percentage of male staff members and teachers compared to other inner city elementary schools at the time, Ms. Brown proved to be the key to propelling that class to greatness. She will always be dear to my heart because without her, the experiment would have died. The single gender classes continued to be the top performing classes every year since they were in third grade. I knew the concept would work because it worked when I was teaching but I needed someone to believe and give it a chance. Ms. Brown produced two years of one hundred percent student attainment and has been one of the top teachers at Coles since her hire. I see a female version of me when I look at Ms. Brown. She is firm but fair and loves kids. Ms. Brown was a true team player. She was just one example of team members stepping up reluctantly but producing greatness as a result of hard work, determination and commitment. We had a dynamic staff. We went from majority white to ninety-nine percent black as a staff and continued to see high results. That was a long way for a principal that was accused of being a racist against his own race. Our beautiful teachers and staff members consistently produced beautiful results as it related to student achievement and overall school improvement. We were a 90/90/90/90 school. We had a more than 90 percent black and brown staff, more than 90 percent free or reduced lunch, more than 90 percent attendance rate and more than 90 percent student growth at an inner city Chicago Public School.

Our students and staff had school pride. For every accomplishment, we had a t-shirt or event to celebrate. I was symbolic of my signature line which reads "If We Highlight Their Strength, The Weaknesses Will Disappear" and sure enough it did, our students increased, naturally, we had less not meeting the standards. My final year, we ordered sweat suits, hoodies and t-shirts that stated "Coles Empire." We truly built an empire of success. I actually got the idea from the Fox Television series *Empire*. I guess you could say I was Lucious Lyon. My Cookie was Ms. Galmore. One of the final student trips under my tenure at Coles was to San Francisco. I ordered Coles Empire gear for all the students and staff participants. It was a sight to see a group of black students and adults walk through O'Hare International airport and San Francisco airport in unison as one unit all dressed in Coles Empire gear from head to toe. We even had Coles socks. Those were proud moments as principal of Coles School. Many of those student trips were possible because of Ms. Galmore. Many people didn't know she would use her own money to secure the student trips and get reimbursed upon our return. She would have up to $7,000.00 of her own money on hold so the students could participate in the experience. That's a true testimony of her heart and what the students meant to us, we made the sacrifices. I didn't know it but I felt like the next challenge in my career was approaching so I really went all out for that graduating class of 2016. That would be my last graduating class as principal of Coles School. Those were the kindergarten students I started with in 2007. We went on a student trip every month, I attended the San Francisco trip with them and I set it up where each graduate's graduation fees were paid by an adult sponsor.

We went out in style at the last graduation under my tenure as we marched in and exited on Beyonce's song "I Was Here" There almost wasn't a clean face in the auditorium, including myself as somehow we knew the Dase-Estes era at Coles School was coming to an end. We closed out the school year as normal and prepared for the opening of another school year as I continued the interview process for Deputy Chief of Schools. During my second interview, the conversation changed from Deputy Chief of Schools to Chief of Schools. I reached out to my mentor at the time to discuss the sudden change and she met me in the parking lot on University of Chicago campus and I recall her saying, "no, you really need to be a Deputy Chief of Schools for at least one year. Chief of Schools is a beast of a position." I was relieved she was in my corner and on the same page as it related to my next step up the leadership ladder with Chicago Public Schools. I wanted to be a Deputy Chief of Schools and learn from an experienced Chief of Schools. On Saturday, August 6, 2016, she, my mentor, called me on my cellular phone and told me she would be recommending me to become Chief of Schools of her former network. She was moving up to lead another department. I immediately said "What?" I was totally against the idea. She stated there was no one else she felt comfortable taking over the network. By the end of the conversation, I recall saying "I'll follow your guidance." On Sunday, August 7, 2016, I received a call offering me the position of Chief of Schools for Network 12, my mentor's former network and the network I was currently serving in as principal with colleagues I would be over now. Due to having the previous communication with my mentor, I was not surprised. The first question I asked was "would I be able to get a Deputy Chief of Schools" to assist me? My mentor had not had a Deputy Chief of Schools to assist her but she was a veteran Chief of Schools. The caller stated "yeah sure, it's in your budget."

I called my girlfriend at the time and informed her. She, being the person who always looked out for me asked several questions. Are they going to give you help? Will you get a Deputy? I told her yes and she gave me her approval and confidence. Not only was she my girlfriend but she is a lifelong friend since college that I value so her approval meant a lot. I walked in my friends, Hershel and Elise house and informed them of the "good" news and that I would have to rearrange my plans to return back to Chicago for training. I was in Atlanta when all this went down. I flew back to Chicago on Tuesday, August 9, 2016 to begin my "training" as a newly appointed Chief of Schools with Chicago Public Schools.

I missed the 2016 Chief of Schools photo due to my being informed the day before I would be a Chief of Schools and flying back on the next day. The photo was taken on Monday. I returned to Chicago on Monday night and attended "training" on Tuesday. I guess that was symbolic of what was to come. The "training" would last the remainder of the week. The following week, I reported to my new office on south Dearborn Street in Chicago. My former Chief and mentor would take her Executive Assistant with her so I was left with an Executive Assistant vacancy. The Executive Assistant for the retired Chief of Teaching and Learning was presented to me as an option, and when I met her, I immediately felt comfortable with her skill set and background to take a chance on her as my Executive Assistant.

This was a sign from my Big Homie above as this would be the beginning of a tight and lasting relationship. Shandrea Bell would be my Executive Assistant as Chief of Schools. Shandrea came from central office, downtown. I came from the school level so we both had a learning curve to get acclimated to the network level. We had some bumps in the road throughout our first year together but after each bump was a smile and eventual laughter. I'm not the easiest person to get along with and I had been through my share of clerks as a principal, so I was patient with the process.

As I analyzed my assignment, I began to search for a Deputy Chief of Schools. I called two of the top principals in the district to see if they would consider or knew of any recommendations. I figured it would be hard to get either one to work for me because either one could run the district themselves as top high school principals. Neither is with the district any longer right now. In the process of searching for candidates, I noticed there was only $55,000.00 in the network budget. I inquired about the money for a Deputy Chief of Schools and the reply was a question, "Do you need all your ISLs?" ISL is the district acronym for Instructional Support Leads or as I called them Leaders. I replied yes and we had an exchange which resulted in me being presented with cutting one of my ISLs or going without a Deputy Chief of Schools. The network was already short ISL support compared to other networks and the impacted employee would have no notice and be unemployed. I decided to keep my ISL position to support schools which meant I would have to go without support. I was misinformed. There was no funding for a Deputy Chief of Schools in my network. Several other new Chief of Schools received Deputy Chief of Schools support. I'm not a complainer, so I began doing the work as Chief of Schools. Even though I had worked with these principals before, I didn't know their work within

125

their schools. I began a learning tour in which I spoke to every school staff before school started back for the school year. I articulated my mission and vision for the network which was basically the same as the previous Chief of Schools; however I expanded from K-8 to Pre-K through 8. I'm a strong believer in providing high- quality early childhood education to serve as a student's educational foundation. I worked in this network as a principal. The philosophy was working for me so why change? Let's continue to master and advance, was my thinking. In one of my very first schools I visited, I saw my former wife in the audience taking it all in. We hadn't spoken or seen each other in 10 years. We both were extremely professional as she continued writing notes while I continued talking. My first year was primarily focused on building relationships with my principals and schools. I attended my first quarterly review, which went well, as I pointed out how the district's School Quality Rating Process (SQRP) gives misrepresentation overall. I asked how a Level 1 or 1+ school can have red data meaning a subgroup of students is not performing well. The facilitator at the time sung my praises for pointing that out. I had successfully completed my first quarterly review.

During the second quarterly review, all the top executive officers of Chicago Public Schools were in attendance. The top executive officers began to ask me questions and at the moment I thought I answered with appropriate knowledge, but from her response and look, I quickly realized I did not. I immediately froze and became fixated on her face as I was listening to her advice and recommendations. About thirty minutes went by and I crashed and burned so horribly, they all got up and left the room. I felt so horrible and defeated, I literally cried in the bathroom. Two executive males tried to comfort this broken down soldier but it didn't help that day. It would take me almost a week to recover from that day, but in my opinion, I did not ever recover from it.

I would go on to have another quarterly review and do much better articulating my leadership actions, but none of the top executives were in attendance that time nor would they return to any other quarterly review of mine as Chief of Schools. In my opinion, that was the day that began my demise as a Chief of Schools with Chicago Public Schools under that administration no matter what I'd accomplish. First impressions last, especially when the initial observer doesn't give you an opportunity to redeem yourself. My first year as Chief of Schools would be filled with ups and downs and I never got a good feeling for the work I was doing. It was difficult providing quality guidance and coaching to 36 schools which included 31 elementary schools and 5 high schools. I initially scheduled monthly meetings with my mentor, but after several cancellations due to busy schedules, they stopped after the new year in January 2017. The school year ended and preliminary school data was released showing a sharp decline in my network school performance. I was once again devastated as this would be my worst year as an administrator when it came to school performance. I felt I let the students, principals, executive officers, everyone down. The first two people I called were my mentor and Dr. Brian Ali, my other mentor. Both were taken back but Dr. Ali said, "what's the plan?' My other mentor seemed devastated as well and told me, well, they are going to want to know your plan to correct, let's get together to map out. That was the worst summer of my career but it brought me focus as I planned to develop my principals and prepare for the sense of urgency. I also felt like I was not prepared for the new role so I took advantage of an opportunity to ask for a leadership coach my second year. I even offered to step down as Chief of Schools to a Deputy Chief of Schools position so I could learn from a veteran Chief of Schools. When I asked about this move headed into my second year as Chief of Schools, the response was "you're getting a Deputy." I did not feel me as a struggling Chief of Schools needed the responsibility of developing another person as it related to being provided a Deputy Chief of Schools.

So I'm headed into my second year as Chief of Schools and my new Deputy Chief of Schools gets placed after a secretive selection process in late August. Despite not wanting a Deputy Chief of Schools over a Leadership Coach, I felt I did get paired with a dynamic leader that would make me better overall in Dr. Christopher Blair. He was a former Academic Officer from

Alabama who had the skill set to be a Chief of Schools but did not know the city of Chicago. A smart and supportive mentor told me to be watchful because they brought him in to be a Chief of Schools. In other words, he might be my replacement. This was another sign that my days might be numbered as Chief of Schools.

We would go on to plan and divide the network evenly for support. During week one, I was able to observe all my schools and plan follow-up visits. This cadence continued throughout the first quarter of the school year. I was finally able to get quality school visits with the support of my Deputy Chief of Schools. The number of schools reduced made a huge difference as it related to being supportive and attentive to the school needs. Fast forward to December of 2017. Dr. Blair pulled me to the side after a Chief/ Deputy meeting and informed me he would be leaving to go back to Alabama. After I picked my mouth up off the floor he explained further. He had been a finalist for a superintendent position and the final candidate selection pulled out so that district doubled back and asked him did he want the position. He accepted. He would be closer to his family and his home roots. The first thing I asked him was did he tell the executive officers that hired him here in Chicago? He said he was requesting a meeting to tell them. To my understanding they found out before the meeting and naturally, they were upset. I get a phone call asking me did I know he was leaving. When did I know he was leaving? I told her exactly when he informed me he was leaving. It's been said the executive officers were upset at me because I did not tell them. I could not tell anything I didn't know and I told him when he told me to tell them. Now my loyalty was being questioned, really? So Dr. Blair leaves and I'm solo as Chief of Schools again. As I said I don't complain and kept it moving, after all, I still had Shandrea, who was my right hand, anyway. I did have a discussion about who I wanted as a Deputy Chief of Schools. I submitted two of my principal's names. One was trying to duplicate another perfect school year after earning a perfect school rating score. The other was trying to sustain two consecutive years as a Level 1+ school in which he brought the school from Level 3. They did not ever interview anyone of them. Again, I kept it moving. One of my goals headed into my first year as Chief of Schools was to implement

Performance Management Sessions aligned to Common Core State Standards based instruction. I did not even get to the starting line my first year but was determined not to repeat that downfall my second year. I would develop and implement 5 week Data Day Sessions with school cohort groups. Principals would report out their school's progress every 5 weeks and the focus was on instructional and student achievement.

Implementation started off rocky even after providing several models and walking principals through the process. It was a major change in the network. I was a principal in the network before and we were not doing Data Driven Instructional Cycles like this. Throughout the school year other professional development areas surfaced as a result of principals being required to articulate what was going on within their school buildings. Some additional professional development areas that surfaced were curriculum design, backwards mapping and SMART goal development and monitoring. I provided professional development aligned with specific strategies for each of these areas of development. I provided systems and structures to monitor the SMART goal action items and/ or plans teachers were submitting. After each data day session, principals would receive at least a one-page summary and action items for improvement. I developed and implemented a rubric aligned with the district's principal competencies used for principal evaluation. By week 20 of 30 weeks, the majority of the network principals were well versed in Data Driven Instruction. It was a professional accomplishment to see the process throughout the entire school year especially considering I had no evaluative assistance throughout the school year. I was responsible for observing each of my 35 principals a minimum of two times during the school year.

I was fortunate enough to acquire the support of one of my original coaches and mentors, Joan Dameron-Crisler. Mrs. Crisler was my supervising principal during my leadership training program known as LAUNCH (Leadership Academy and Urban Network for Chicago). When I was asked if I knew of anyone that could assist me with monitoring the schools, I immediately thought of her as I was informed she was one of the retired principals helping out the school district with various areas of administrative support. She proved to be an asset to me and the network as I was able to separate the monitoring tasks once again among two of us instead of one of me. Principals were reluctant at first but after the first month, she had won them over and they were singing her praises. She has a leadership skill set and approach that if you don't see improvement you don't want improvement because you are not trying. She would attend meetings, data day session and check-in with me weekly. I was able to ask her to shadow me and give me some feedback on how I could improve. Finally, I had the closest thing to a coach which is what I had been asking for and seeking as a Chief of Schools. This was full circle for me as the same woman who'd pushed me to become a dynamic leader was the same woman molding me to become a dynamic executive leader.

Fast forward to June 13, 2018. I finally connect with my mentor about a meeting I requested with her to discuss several topics which included improved communication from last school year, areas of development, documentation of professional practices, measuring my effectiveness as a Chief of Schools, lack of professional growth as a Chief of Schools, perception by other senior executive officers, specifically, my boss, corrective actions against specific principals, bogus feelings as it relates to principals running to higher ups about my leadership, principals feeling comfortable running to higher ups about my leadership, data day process and ratings, Deputy Chief inequalities and how we need to resolve for my sanity and other opportunities for professional growth such as an Assistant Superintendent or a district position that supports professional growth. Now all of what I just listed is from a text message I sent to my mentor to review before our meeting to maximize time. When we met, we discussed all these topics and she asked me about my professional support from the district. I told her that with the exception of Dr. Saffold and Dr. Ali, I had no district support. I informed her I had been observed once in my two years as Chief of Schools and I had received no written feedback from that one observation which occurred in May of 2018. I informed her I was thinking about applying for positions outside the district that would support me in my professional growth. She stated she wanted to keep me in the district; however she didn't think the Chief of Schools position was right for me at this time because too many principals are complaining. She went on to say that the complaints were from principals' voices who they value. I was like damn, what about my voice? You all put me in this position. You all know my background. Now my voice is not valued? I was on the same consultant committee these complaining principals are on. Too many hide behind the committee while doing the bare minimum to increase student achievement. People complain with accountability. She asked me what I am asking them to do because they just keep saying it's too much. I'm thinking well maybe if someone comes out and observed what I'm doing you all would know. Hell, I even asked for unannounced observations and received none.

She asked me did I think I was prepared for the position. I said, "No, but I've grown and I have my groove right now." She told me that I have a good reputation in the district and she doesn't want that tarnished so what other positions would I consider. We discussed the master principal position which came with a principal salary and a signing bonus of $15,000.00 to support other principals. We discussed the newly created Network Operations Manager position but the initial salary discussed was too low and she didn't want me to take a deep cut in pay. I left that meeting actually feeling good because once again, I took it as my mentor looking out for me. I paid the bill; we laughed, hugged and parted ways.

We closed out the school year with a bang.. Our last principal and assistant principal meeting was combined as a network administrator's softball game. We selected two enthusiastic principal captains that organized a day filled with barbeque, smack talk and fun. Naturally, the team I was on won this inaugural game as everyone had a great time and we decided to start a tradition as this would be our annual principal and assistant principal end of the year softball game. Besides our network awards event, this was another event that brought us closer as a network family in which everyone wanted the best for everybody. With the preliminary student achievement scores up and everyone leaving with all smiles,

I felt good about entering into my third year as Chief of Schools for Chicago Public Schools. As June ended and July began, I began completing my required 35 principal summative evaluations. This year was much smoother than the last school year as I changed my approach. I sent everything to the principals ahead of time to review and question unlike last school year when they arrived to the meeting and the initial discussion occurred then. The majority of the meetings were short and there was very little push back from principals. They had received feedback throughout the school year so there were very few surprises. There were very few but there were some. Of course, I had to deal with the mediocre principal who thought he was distinguished. One meeting was so sad, the principal began an attempt to negotiate her final rating but still ended up with a Basic she arrived with given a few extra points overall. When you hold people accountable, pushback and disagreements come with the territory. I finally finished my last principal evaluation as I was preparing to go on vacation the following week. During the week in question, I noticed a calendar invite titled Jeffery Dase Network Chief Evaluation for Thursday, July 26, 2018 at 3:30 p.m. This was scheduled right after a follow-up meeting I would have with my boss and several principals that had been complaining about their principal observation and evaluation ratings. This follow up meeting literally took six months to schedule and complete. As my boss schedule kept conflicting with the complaining principals' schedules, there were multiple changes in dates and times. Hell, I just thought she was prolonging the garbage complaints but anyhow, it was finally scheduled. So, I finish the last of my 35 principal evaluations on July 25, 2018 around 3:00 p.m. I got up the next morning and attend a Chicago Public Schools and DIVVY Bike Tour event at one of my schools and went home in the afternoon to change into a suit to attend these last two meetings with my boss before I go on vacation. Coincidence, my last principal observation, evaluation and school engagement activity as Chief of Schools was with the same principal, Dr. David Young of Bouchet Elementary School who I had grown to admire as a person beyond the principal position. My July plan was working just fine. As I arrived to the follow-up meeting, I noticed there's only one principal present. My thoughts at the time were, yeah, the other one knew it was some garbage so he pulled out of the meeting.

Now the meeting was with me, my boss and the female principal. My boss allowed her to go first and tell her accounts as to why she disagreed with her principal and evaluation rating. Of course I'm on the other side of this complaint and I would say everything out of her mouth was a lie and personal but really, everything out her mouth was a lie and personal. She had the audacity to say I didn't compliment her after her school gave a good presentation at one of the previous high school meetings. She stated that everyone else gave her compliments except me which proved I had something against her. She also said that I don't ever smile at her which is proof I don't like her. She began to get emotional and almost cried before my boss allowed me to say my comments. I was brief as I began with "she's a liar." My boss immediately corrected me and said I couldn't call her that. I asked her how she can come into this meeting and present emotional, sensitive opinions as grounds for filing a complaint against me. We went back and forth briefly again before my boss asked me was it some items that I rated her on that I didn't rate other principals on? I said no, all elementary school principals were rated using the same criteria as were all high school principals were rated using the same criteria. I offered an apology to my female principal if any of my leadership actions came off as personal and non-professional. She began to get emotional again saying irrelevant comments but ended with she felt like I was threatening her job. I made the statement "I'm glad we are here." She asked me are you threatening me. I told her I was referring to us having this meeting to clear the air and resolve any dispute. At that time my boss put her hands on her shoulder and escorted her out of the room into the hallway while my female principal is saying she's getting a lawyer. As my boss walks her out I overhear her saying, don't worry this will be taken care of. That would become a key statement as she returned into the room for our Chief Evaluation meeting.

She returned into the room and asked me about the school year and why I rated myself the way I did on multiple categories of the self-assessment I completed and submitted to her prior to this meeting.

After I finished, she asked me the question "Do you feel you have improved your communication and formed good relationships with your principals to remain Chief of Schools?" Before I answered, I sat back in the chair because I knew then where this was going and said "Yes!" She stated "well, I would have needed your data to go up in a few more areas to keep you as an elementary Chief of Schools for a third year. I said "Wow, really, what data are you referring to?"

Important Note: While she was saying this, she had no data in front of her, there was no data present, and we did not review any data during the meeting.

She asked me how I felt about that. I told her "it's a mistake but the decision has been made so if I'm not going to be an elementary Chief of Schools, what are my options?" She briefly mumbled about the master principal position and named two possible schools I could be placed at. She also stated I would be an asset at the high school level, however, I need to update my high school experience. She was so short with her words, I immediately knew she was not the decision maker, she was the deliverer. She was so uncomfortable delivering that message that she told me to think about it and to give her a call Monday all while she was exiting the doorway. I remained in the room, looking at the walls for at least 10 minutes after her race car exit thinking, damn, what just happened?

What just happened was I was about to transition from my Chief of Schools position into limbo, no title, no defined position but the Lord is good. I'm still on the payroll. They wanted to inform me of the decision because the Chief and Deputy Chief of Schools boot camp was beginning the following Monday. My boss informed me I didn't have to attend. It was at this point a little anger crept into my soul, particularly at my mentor. From June 13th to July 26th, more than one month in between the dates, I had absolutely no communication with any senior executive officer, specifically my mentor or boss, so as the school year ended and the new fiscal year began, I began planning for an even better third year as Chief of Schools. Sure, we had an "off the record" conversation between mentor and mentee but to have this happen without any communication, yeah, I was beyond pissed. After all, I requested the June 13th meeting with my mentor. No one requested to meet with me to discuss my progress or lack of progress if that was the case. At least I had some insight into how my mentor felt after the meeting but other than that, there was no communication. I left that meeting with hopes of more support for the overall Chief of Schools position and some communication about my next steps but when that didn't occur and with improved student achievement results, I just knew I was secure in my position for another school year. I have always requested face-to-face conversations and for her to make this decision with no further communication with me just plain and simple, hurt. I felt like she threw me away when she knew for herself, the district does a poor job in preparing and supporting the position. If a student performs poorly, we look at the teacher. If a teacher performs poorly, we look at the principal. If a Chief performs poorly, we look around, not at the senior leadership responsible for his/ her development. I became a good Chief of Schools with little support. I transitioned before becoming great. I worked my butt off for 21 years for Chicago Public Schools and our students, made an impact and this was the result. I was in utter disbelief. I was not upset at the decision because I took to heart the higher you move up the more at-will you are and you can transition at any time. It was how the decision was handled and delivered. I thought I earned a more formal approach than what I received. I did not get that. Lesson learned but I don't judge an entire organization by the actions of a few. Those who know me and my work ethic within Chicago Public Schools know this was a wrong decision but just like I have done throughout my life, the decision provided me motivation to do bigger and better things in my life and the lives of students within Chicago Public Schools. I decided not to leave the district because had I left, that would have gone against my creed that I'm here for the students, not the adults overall. Yes, I love many of the adults in the organization but my worth, my legacy will live on through the students of Chicago Public Schools that I help to become productive citizens in society. No one person or one decision will ever determine my worth. After 21 stellar years, the second half of my career began on Friday, July 27, 2018.

I was scheduled to go out of town that following Tuesday so my mind immediately shifted to securing my next position before I left out of town. It was Thursday, so I had four days to work some magic so I wouldn't have a horrible vacation. After I left the downtown CPS office, the first person I called was Shandrea and told her we need to talk. She was at the 31st Street Pier. I drove to Jewel's on 35th Street, bought a bottle of Sangria, walked across the bridge and told her the breaking news. She was devastated. We talked, drank and just stared in disbelief most of the night. Right around this time, Kelly Cooper, Eboni's sister had died suddenly in her sleep and I was there comforting her and her family while handling my setback also. Being around them actually helped me cope with my emotions. Just when you think you have it bad, there is something worst and Kelly's death was devastating to Eboni and her family.

The next day, I attended a scheduled vendor presentation with my network team as only me and Shandrea knew the breaking news. We completed the meeting and had our end of the year network lunch as Ja'Grill in Hyde Park. I laughed and joked with my network family which included Mrs. Crisler. After lunch, I walked Mrs. Crisler to her car and informed her of the decision. Needless to say, she was devastated. We talked for a while then she wished me a great vacation as we parted ways. I did ask her to reach out to one of the CPS OGs for me as I knew she could assist me and was an advocate for me. I spoke to Dr. Saffold and Dr. Ali that day; after all, I felt out of respect, I had to tell them. To my surprise, they both had no clue. Seems as if the decision was a two-woman, maybe three-woman decision, but definitely two-woman. The next day, Shandrea checks on me, she is still pissed. She tells me to call the OG. I refused at first but finally I did. That was one of the best decisions I have made because things started to move with that one phone call. When I finally called the OG, she was genuinely upset at the developments as it related to my transition from the Chief of Schools position. She asked me what had taken place and what communication had I received prior to the decision. I told her about the meeting I had previously with my mentor and the meeting with my boss when she told me I would transition from the Chief of Schools position. Again, my bitterness was not about the decision but the cowardly delivery. Had I been warned about conflicts with my leadership and given opportunities to improve and I did not then no way would I be surprised but that communication, observations, support did not take place. I talked to the OG three times that day and each time she guided me through my next steps as it related to communication with my mentor and next step career options. She was the one that told me I'm an asset to the district. She shared with me past stories from her professional career that helped my feelings at the time. She convinced me to call my mentor and start the communication so I did just that. I called and left my mentor a message. I texted her to call me when time permitted. She texted me back that she was at a district retreat and would call me back. She called me back several hours later. The conversation was totally focused on my next steps career-wise with the district. The elementary Chief of Schools boat had sailed and there was no discussion on that matter. She brought up the high school Network Operations Manager position and explained it would provide me an opportunity to become current with the high school systems and structures and eventually lead to the high school Chief of Schools, then she threw out a salary. Well the salary was higher than I had expected so I immediately said, well, if you can work that out for me I would greatly appreciate it. Although the salary was less than my Chief of Schools salary, it was more than I was making when I left my principal position which was where my minimum salary request was at the time. That allowed me to avoid a lifestyle setback/pay cut because ever since I was assistant principal I have always lived off the previous position salary. When I was an assistant principal, I lived off what I made as a teacher, saved and invested the difference. When I was a principal, I lived off what I made as an assistant principal, saved and invested the difference. When I was a Chief of Schools, I lived off what I made as a principal, saved and invested the difference. I was not ever use to living off my Chief of Schools salary therefore the pay cut did not hurt me or my lifestyle. I don't spend the promotion money until I get another promotion. Basically, I lived off principal salary as Chief of Schools which I am continuing now since the Network Operations Manager position pays more than my previous principal salary. I will continue this until my next promotion which will come, whether with my current district or another district throughout the nation. My mentor called me back that evening and confirmed my new position with the district. Before we got off the phone together, I asked her for a meeting after all this blew over because I needed clarity as to why the decision was made and what I need to do to move back up the ranks within the school district. She gave me her word this meeting would take place and was a must for my future with the district.

That communication was on Monday, July 30, 2018. Shortly after talking to her, my boss called and confirmed my new position with the district. Before we got off the phone, I asked her for the same meeting I'd asked my mentor for as it related to clarity around the decision and support in moving up the ranks again within the district. She too, was receptive to the offer and ensured me the meeting would take place. On Tuesday, August 1, 2018, I boarded a plane to New Orleans and would take a two-week vacation. Lord knows I needed that time for myself and to enjoy my family and friends. I would enjoy the two weeks visiting family in Georgia and Mississippi and also enjoying friends during my 25th Class Reunion

(Percy L. Julian High School) in New Orleans before finishing my vacation in the exotic Dominican Republic. That was a great ending to a two week vacation. It was filled with fun, rest and relaxation. It literally was the first time in over 20 years I could 100% enjoy my vacation without thinking about work. I had no defined responsibilities so I had nothing to prepare for. It felt great. Every individual I crossed paths with during those two weeks helped me through this transition. I'm grateful for them all. Once again, the Lord is great!

It's also important to know that I two of my closest friends during this chapter of my life when I was assistant principal at Julian High School, which are Lorenzo Russell and Lonnie Felters. Majority of my current friendships were formed during this chapter of my life. I developed a tight bond with friends such as Kevin Wilks, Marcus Garner aka Poon, Alfred Mayes, III aka Al Esquire, Todd aka Famo, Shane, Leon aka the Comedian, Lil Man, Boosie, Spunk, Mook, Mario, Latrez Clements aka Trez and their families. One thing I'm proud of is that all of us take care of our responsibilities as fathers.

Another proud moment was when Trez enrolled his son Marcus in Coles when I was a school principal. That was priceless to have your friend entrust you with his son's education. Marcus was one of my best students ever. Speaking of Marcus, my Boi Marcus Garner aka Poon gave me some of the best motivational quotes during my tenure as a principal. If you go into Coles today, his motivational quotes are still on the walls of the school. My friends may not be in the field of education, but they have supported, encouraged and inspired my career in education throughout the years.

My village may seem large from all the names, but my village is a tight circle of genuine and caring individuals that I trust. It should be noted that it was one of my incidents that bonded us all. On February 1, 2004 while celebrating Simone's birthday and watching the New England Patriots beat the Carolina Panthers in Super Bowl XXXVIII, I encountered one of the racist moments in my life. After the game, as I was walking up the stairs with Corey to go to our cars and go home, I noticed a nice looking female and asked, "do you have a significant other?" Without hesitation she replied, "Oh my god, a nigga spoke to me" and smacked me. I immediately became upset and had some choice words for her that I would not say in front of my mother or daughter. She proceeded to call the Blue Island Police Department. As we get in our cars and pull off for the night, the police arrive, draw their guns on our cars and block our exit to drive off. The police go into the venue and talk to the female. The police come out, place me in handcuffs and in the back of one of their squad cars. The female told the police I hit her. As I'm sitting in the back of the squad car, I see my life flash before me. As I looked out the right-side window of the squad car, I noticed an elderly couple talking to the police. After they finished talking, the police officer comes around to my side of the squad car, opens the door and let me out. As he is unlocking the handcuffs, he says "this is your lucky night." The elder couple had witnessed the female smack me and told the police the truth. The elder couple literally saved my life that night. Had I been arrested that night; my life would have been forever altered. My friends and I bonded that night, especially myself and Shane. As I was saying "I didn't do anything wrong" Shane being one of the older friends with more wisdom constantly stated, "you don't need this Bro, you have too much to lose." This would mark the second time in my life I was almost arrested on February 1st. I stay in on February 1st nowadays.

CHAPTER 7

Closed Door Opens an Overflow of Blessings

Upon my return to the United States, Chicago and Chicago Public Schools, I was still employed in the Chief of Schools title. As I reviewed past text and missed messages some people were asking what's going on, some were sending condolences text messages like I had died or something. With all this going on I assumed my boss informed my Chief of Schools colleagues about the transition. After all, the two week Chief-Deputy Boot Camp training for Chief of Schools and Deputy Chief of Schools had taken place which included sessions with your network team. I decided to send out a see you around and thank you text to the other Chief of Schools on our Chief of Schools Group Me text thread.

Within a minute of my hitting send, I begin to get text messages and emails from Chief of Schools asking what is going on. I realized then they did not know. After two weeks together, the Chief of Schools did not know who the new Chief of Schools were yet. The network teams did not know who their Chief of Schools was yet. I was in utter disbelief so I called my partner and she informed me "Jeff, they didn't tell anybody." I stopped all communication after that moment until the district announced the new Chief of Schools for each network. The outpour of support, encouragement and bitterness from some lasted almost two months. People wanted me to leave. Groups wanted to rally and protest but I kept telling everyone, it's cool; I'm okay which I was considering the circumstances. Of course there were rumors on both sides as it related to me being at fault and the district being at fault. I can honestly say I felt proud of the support and encouragement I received from colleagues and friends. My family still has no clue because that's not what they care about. As long as I'm able to still take care of myself and I'm safe, that's all that matters to my family.

Some of the most genuine support came from my best friend Clarence. When first told, he said he was not worried about me but that he was scared of what I was going to do next that excited him the most meaning he knew this transition would motivate me to do bigger and better things. He asked me once was I good? When I said yes, he left it alone and we continued to enjoy life that weekend. We were in New Orleans. Another time was when I and my friend Devona went out to lunch and she told me that people were still singing my praises and saying I was a good dude over five months after the transition occurred. That was confirmation I was doing right in my position as Chief of Schools and before then. I appreciated how the genuine people supported Jeff Dase and not the Chief of Schools. Many people will be around for your status or title, few will be around just for you but I had a lot people that were around for me, regardless of my title and that was self-rewarding and confirmation I was doing right by people. This was not ever more evident than on Thursday, October 4, 2018 when I received the Trailblazer Award from Kenwood High School Brotherhood, Inc. at their 2nd Annual Fundraiser Gala. When I received my award, I was allowed to give a brief speech and I thanked all those in attendance for supporting me. When I asked all my supporters in attendance to stand to give them recognition, literally over half the room stood up, including my boss that delivered the message I was being transitioned from the Chief of Schools position. It was an amazing sight and an amazing night. The founder and director of Kenwood Brotherhood, Inc. Dr. Shelby Wyatt told me he would honor me the next year because they sold the most tickets to my supporters. He was joking about honoring me again but serious about my supporters buying the most tickets.

From August to December, I would get acclimated to the new position while still enduring the occasional question of "are you all right" from individuals. I took it as a blessing that people still cared about me as an individual to ask. I mastered certain responses like, "Yes, you know how we do; we keep it moving" and "still standing." I would also use "I'm alive, I'm good" from time to time but basically let everyone know that I'm good, no bitterness about the decision and still wouldn't let on that I was bitter about the delivery. I had groups write letters and even attend the Chicago Board of Education monthly meeting and express their support for me and my work. I had principals wanting to protest but I told them, that would only get them in trouble and no one needs to get in trouble over this except the one who make the decision if it was improper. I wasn't in trouble so why pull someone else in on drama I didn't or they didn't create. It didn't make sense to me so I told everyone to stand down. I took it as a message from God to slow down. I had been grinding hard for Chicago Public Schools for over 20 years. I was fortunate enough to raise a beautiful daughter over those years but the grind did have an impact on my personal life. Those who are not in it rarely understand the sacrifices it takes to be really good in the field of education. You may have time for one more aspect of life and for me, it was my daughter but my relationships took a hit in the meantime. I was in and out of relationships with multiple women, not willing to commit because I didn't have the time. I wanted to be great in my career and as a dad and that left little room to be great as a boyfriend or mate. I had difficulty balancing the three and when difficult times came, the relationship was the easiest to let go because the career paid me and fatherhood, letting that go was a non-negotiable. It was unfortunate because I had some great women in my life. I made sacrifices but I also enjoyed life as well. I have few regrets in life and I have been blessed throughout life to enjoy it. I have been able to travel internationally, have memorable moments with family and friends and help others along the way. All this has been possible though the payments from Chicago Public Schools for my services. Even now, with a pay cut and transition, I still make more than many around the world, so I'm grateful to Chicago Public Schools and all those that have blessed me with opportunities.

That being said, nothing makes unfair practices acceptable. Too many people accept monetary benefits to ignore unfair practices. Right is right, wrong is wrong. Is it going to change anything for them to admit they were wrong transitioning me from the Chief of Schools position? No. The damage has been done, but it will provide some satisfaction that I feel I'm owed, especially from those that said they supported me but transitioned me without just cause. This transition also provided me with opportunities for some "me" time. I'm able to continue my monthly personal traveling, have more availability on the weekends for personal time and time to write this book which is a personal goal of mine. I'm using this transition year as personal rebuilding time, which ultimately will make me better as a professional. I'm a man of strong faith and for the first time in my life I'm on track to attend church every Sunday since March 2018. Even with my travels, I make time to attend the nearby church of worship. I'm in the process of building a better body, a better person, a better Jeff Dase. I may even be ready to build a better relationship as it relates to long term and eventually marriage. My buddy Dr. Richadine Murry would laugh at that statement because every time she sees me she asks me where my wife is. She has been a constant support and encouragement to me since I met her at Julian High School. I know one thing, I have used more vacation days this school year than any other year I've worked with Chicago Public Schools. They originally told me I have five weeks per school year. I might run out this school year. I call them rejuvenation days. When I know I have a trip coming each month, I work harder to get to that day ultimately making me more productive for the district. Vacation days help us all.

The school year began and it took several months for principals and network staff to accept the transition but I would always advise them to give their all and support their new Chief of Schools. She is a sharp and strong lady that I have known for years and support as a leader. Many wanted to bait me into talking badly about her--not going to happen. She didn't make the decision. She just benefitted from the decision. No harm, no foul towards me from her and I wish her the best. I was disappointed the transition did not allow the network to have the 3rd annual awards event because with all the positive progress there was sure to be more competition and suspense as schools were looking to dethrone Dixon School as the School of the Year. Not only did Dixon School win School of the Year but they earned a perfect school rating score of 5.0 the previous school year which was a result of outstanding school and student performance under the leadership of Principal Terrycita Perry. I was particularly impressed by Parkside, Bouchet, Mann and Tanner Schools to compete for awards this year. Several principals who had been discussed for Corrective Action Plans (CAPs) moved their schools up one or two levels which was important to me as well.

I've always said you have to build a solid relationship to get others to work for you. For some, it's more intrinsic but for those who lack that intrinsic side mostly, you have to build and coach their capacity to produce. It took the entire two years for some but unfortunately, we were separated before we could continue into year three. We had already said our theme for school year 2019 was "Get Up and Stay Up!" This was a result of too many schools being inconsistent. One year they would be up, the next year they would fall. We were determined to maintain the best network status for years to come. The new school year has provided me the opportunities to work with some dynamic school leaders. I was worried about working on the city of Chicago Westside but we have the least amount of complaints and principals handle things in house which is a blessing to any Chief of Schools and Operations Manager, especially if you are new. My Chief of Schools, Randel Josserand, is a great man who allows you to do your job without micro-managing. He is definitely not a title man and works with our network team to solve and improve school outcomes. I feel blessed to have landed with him as my Chief of Schools.

That is a story in itself also. The first time I was asked to select my place of employment. I was told to reach out to the two Chief of Schools, interview with them and decide which one I would be a best fit with. I reached out to them, interviewed with both and the interview was a cross between a sympathy and empathy. Both clearly felt bad for me as it related to me transitioning from the Chief of Schools position. Both wanted the best for me which I respected whole heartedly. I informed them that even though the decision is being put in my hand, I didn't feel comfortable selecting my place of employment. They should have asked me during that meeting with my boss; I would have said I want to be placed as a Chief of Schools in Network 12. Wishful thinking, so I was originally placed as Network Operations Manager in Network 16 on the south side of Chicago. I figured they placed me there because I live on the south side and would not have to travel far to my schools. On the first day of training for the new position, something was stated to one of my supervisors and I was told to reach out to my current Chief of Schools to see if I wanted to work with him. I followed the directive, had a great feeling after the conversation and the next day I was Network Operations Manager of Network 15 under the leadership of Chief of Schools Randel Josserand. Keep in mind on day one of the training they presented me with all Network 16 data. Within a day I had switched networks. I have a screen shot that says I was in Network 16 so technically; I worked for two networks this school year as Operations Manager. Again, I'm a man of strong faith and He guided me and blessed me to land under the leadership of Chief of Schools Randel Josserand. Many people, including myself, think this was a calculated move to get me more experience and then move me up to a high school Chief of Schools. I'm looking forward to my clarification meeting so I can get some clarity on my future with this school district. In the meantime, I have to exercise my options because it has become difficult to trust solely off verbal words lately.

Along with a great man as a Chief of Schools, I've been blessed with assistance from retired administrators such as Anthony Spivey and Eugene Crawford. Our team of Network Operation Managers is awesome as well. We work well together. I'm sure they get frustrated with me and my schedule as I have been absent from many meetings this school year due to my participation in the Chicago Urban League IMPACT Leadership Program. IMPACT stands for Informed – Motivated – Perceptive – Authentic – Connected – Talent. It's a program that prepares black leaders to uplift and enhance our communities throughout Chicago. It was approved participation by my former boss. She probably approved because she didn't think I would get accepted. God is Great! As a team, we are writing and defining the position of Network Operations Manager this school year for a better roll out next school year. We have embraced the role as the position is new for us all this school year. Anthony and Eugene have previous experience in similar roles for the district so they have been an invaluable asset to us all in the inaugural year of the position. Somehow the label of Lead NOM (Network Operations Manager) was laid on me but no one ever defined what a Lead NOM does so I have been reluctant but cooperative without guidance. My take is, I was leading and was transitioned, now you all are charging me with leading another team with no clear defined description of what that is. I'm still looking for clarity as it relates to what to do and not to do aligned to my leadership and in the meantime, I'm charged with leading another team of individuals. I can do it but we continue to repeat the pattern of unpreparedness which is frustrating when you are trying to be a catalyst to move a district forward.

Re: Meeting Request - Jeff Dase

Sat, Nov 3, 2018, 12:01 AM

Good evening Chief ██████,

I know your schedule is extremely busy. I am following up on our previous conversation. If at all possible can we schedule a date and time to meet with all parties we discussed for this meeting.

Nov 3, 2018, 5:29 AM

Good Morning,

Yes, I will get it scheduled within the next two weeks before the Thanksgiving holiday.

Hope all is well with you,

██████

██████
██████

Chicago Public Schools

42 West Madison Street

Chicago, IL 60602

██████

Twitter: @CPSTeachLearn

Thanksgiving break … no meeting.

Winter/ Christmas break … no meeting.

Let's look at the data.

"The Decision"

Network Level Breakdown by Overall School Performance

Network	Increased	Decreased	Maintained	Chief Status
	5	14	25	Left District (Promotion)
	9	2	8	Left District (Promotion)
	6	6	6	Promoted to HS Chief of Schools
	4	6	17	Retained as ES Chief of Schools
	9	9	7	Retained as ES Chief of Schools
	3	8	8	Left District (Unknown)
	5	6	6	Retained as ES Chief of Schools

	6	5	7	Retained as ES Chief of Schools
	5	5	11	Retained as ES Chief of Schools
	8	6	14	Retained as ES Chief of Schools
	6	13	12	Promoted to HS Chief of Schools
12*	10	7	12	Transitioned from Chief of Schools
	7	13	12	Retained as ES Chief of Schools

* Network 12 School Level Breakdown

(2017-2018 School Performance)

Level 1+ Schools: 10
Level 1 Schools: 4
Level 2+ Schools: 10
Level 2 Schools: 6
Level 3 Schools: 0

Hmm … maybe there has not been a meeting because it's difficult

to explain why you decided to transition the Chief of Schools that had the best overall school performance the previous school year. December 2018 was the first time I sat down and analyzed the school performance data. My plans were simply to discuss the "why" and my next steps with this district had a meeting taken place before now. I knew I had a good year as it related to school performance but I didn't know I had a good year compared to other networks. Now, the bitterness intensifies a little as I see how my network outperformed other networks and I'm the only Chief of Schools that was transitioned from the position. The current Chief Executive Officer (CEO) and Chief Education Officer (CEDO) solicited me for this position. How can I be transitioned with these results? Unbelievable. I have asked three times for clarity and no meeting so at this point, I'm convinced, the meeting is not priority and will not happen so my only voice is to continue to write. This is my voice. The district is committed to building the capacity of its leaders but my capacity gets immediately halted when it's looking promising. That's not what this administration is about. Now the why intensifies. Why was this decision made? Am I a "risk" for having another stellar year which is what the district needs to grow?

All throughout this school year, the Lord has sent me signs that I'm doing the right thing by expressing myself via this written communication. Again, the transition has given me more of a life-work balance. I have been able to escape the city of Chicago every month so far which continues my streak since my second year as Chief of Schools. I was blessed to celebrate Christmas with my daughter Jakia. Her birthday is on Christmas Eve so we celebrated her birthday and Christmas in Las Vegas this year. It was the first time we've celebrated either day out of town. Upon my return, I stayed in Chicago for a couple of days and then headed to Atlanta for my friends annual New Year's Eve Party. After Christmas break, I worked for several days and then headed to Cuba on a planned cruise with the Julian High School Class of 1994. It was one of the most memorable times of my life. I don't usually have to revisit certain destinations but I will definitely revisit Cuba. The class of 1994 really knows how to enjoy life. I got a chance to kick it with my Gyrl Dawn and all the other class of 1994 classmates that attended. Three vacations within three weeks -- yeah, I was living my best life.

Upon returning to work, I sat down with my Chief of Schools and we had another real discussion and school performance data became a topic of discussion. I told him I finally sat down and reviewed my school performance data from my last year as Chief of Schools. He told me he had reviewed and analyzed the data also. During the discussion, we both became pissed thinking about me being transitioned. He even went on to confirm that several other Chief of Schools had performed worse than me for several years and they still are Chief of Schools. It just confirmed there was no real rationale for the decision.

Time goes on and we are about to end the first semester of school year 2019. Our attendance data for the network is down. Our freshmen on-track data is down. Our sophomore on-track data is down. We map out action plans to get in front of principals. Chief has team meetings with the principals. He sets up the sense of urgency and I come behind to seal the deal as it relates to principals owning the action steps and improvement plans. I have been completing my duties as an Operations Manager along with participating on instructional core visits, post-secondary meetings and leading attendance improvement efforts. I inform Chief that is he wants me to increase the attendance in our network something else is going to fall by the waist side because attendance improvement is a huge overhaul. I mapped out an attendance improvement action plan with our network team and when I realized the time and effort it would take to effectively develop and monitor, I realized once again my talents were about to be wasted. I was becoming an attendance monitor. Despite feeling this way, I still found time to interact and engage with the students and staff at the schools I visited. I had a chance during this time to visit Gage Park during a professional development session. This was a rewarding experience because I had a chance to observe the school principal provide professional development to her staff. It was rewarding because the principal is my former teacher from Coles School. The assistant principal is one of my former Coles teachers as well.

We had an opportunity to talk briefly and she told me the strategies I had them doing at Coles was working at the high school level. That comment in itself was confirmation that we did good at Coles and our leadership still lives on beyond us. That's true leadership. We transferred skills and best practices that live on through the countless leaders we've mentored over the years. During that brief meeting, she pulled me into her office and told me "look, I'm telling you something and I just want you to reflect, don't get mad." She told me people were discussing my Boi being removed from his position as principal. She said she felt uncomfortable not saying anything but if she had they would not say anything else around her if they knew she knew me like that. I thanked her for telling me because a lot of times people remain silent about others talking behind your back.

Speaking of my Boi, I finally talked to him face to face and bottom line, I wanted to know was he okay and where his mind was at the time. There were all types of rumors but I'm not the judge or the jury and I just wish the best for him and I'm hopeful for his return. That was the only probing question I asked him, does it look like you can return. Regardless of what happened, this brother has a good heart. We have had plenty one-on-one conversations about the work and life. This brother is a good human being. Sure, we all make mistakes. I don't crucify anyone. That's not my place on this earth. People have forgiven me for mistakes I have made in life and I am here today reaping the benefits of a second chance. I try to extend the same to others. We had a great face-to-face conversation. That was the first time I spent the night over his house. It was mandatory after our one-on-one session. I can't remember Scotch going so fast before. The work, life balance gives me time to plan for myself and Clarence 30 years of friendship trip. I get emotional every time I think of us being friends for 30 years. We have had our trials but the good by far outweighs the bad and we have a bond like no other. He's my friend, my brother, my family.

I have also entered the world of social media in 2019. I joined Twitter to promote my work in the education field, specifically mentoring and increasing overall performance of black males. I have my Gyrl assisting me with navigating the social media platforms. She put me on a 100 followers quota before I could start another social media account such as Facebook or Snapchat. All should be useful in promoting my mentoring and public speaking platform. I have also started a Jeff Dase Positive Platform in which I'm trying to recruit all positive individuals on an uplift mission to increase the social and emotional well-being of people but specifically black folks. This was inspired by my friends Kiesha, Amadeus and Ali. When I was promoted to Chief of Schools, I began receiving daily inspirational Bible scriptures and/ or messages from my friend Kiesha. Now she may miss one day here and there but she has literally kept this up for nearly three years now. These motivational scriptures and messages kept me motivated throughout the last three years and the fact that she continued despite me sometimes not replying for a week meant the world to me. I call her my Angel. During my second year as Chief of Schools, I was reunited with my Bio Amadeus. I remembered Amadeus from our first encounter and we just had a genuine vibe for each other. We met up again and just smiled and hugged each other as he introduced me to his family and I told everyone we had met before. We exchanged contact information and since we reunited, he has sent me motivational scriptures and message every Sunday. Just like Kiesha's messages,

Amadeus messages have motivated me and kept me inspired over the past year. After my job title transition, a long-time friend named Ali began sending me scriptures every week that have been inspirational. These are three positive individuals that I have been blessed to have in my life are motivational and inspirational. Most people have one person, but two or three, that's a true blessing and for them to stay consistent with the positive messages is unbelievable to me but I believe it and they have inspired me to be a positive influence in more people lives which is why I wanted to start the Jeff Dase Positive Platform. I want to spread the gratitude that has been extended to me to enlighten another person's day, week, year and/ or life. This is me giving back what has been given to me. Throughout this phase of my life over the last year, I have been blessed with positive individuals in my life. Another example is my Bio, Sylus. Sylus is the photographer that helped me design my book cover and marketing items. I met Sylus at the Network 12 Back to School Bash in August 2018. I was in amazement by his 5:30 Scholars Program and his talented kids who were challenging each other on Greek and Latin words. I ran into Sylus again at the photo shoot for our Men of Color in Education mentoring group meeting at Truman College. We talked and I told him about my first photographer and how he disappeared with my photos after I paid him in full. He told me to call him and we could set up a date and time for him to complete a photo shoot for me.

We finally scheduled a date and time which was the coldest day of the year, a record breaking day for Chicago. We met at the new Pullman Community Center. We started at two o'clock and did not leave until close to eight o'clock that evening. He had to shoot around two hundred shots that day and he sat me down for a video shoot. After the day was over, he shook my hand and said have a great evening. He would not charge me one dime for this five to six hour photo shoot session. My mouth almost hit the floor. I looked up and thanked God once again for the positive people he put in my path. Sylus went on to say he just wanted to support a brother's effort and that he was excited for me which is why he volunteered to help me with the photo shoot opportunity. Even though I met Sylus on my own, I met him again through my good friend Shawn.

Dr. Shawn Jackson, President of Truman College in Chicago. I say this to point out the importance of networking and not burning bridges. We all are one positive comment from another positive opportunity or outcome. We all are also one negative comment from a lost opportunity or negative outcome. Try to stay positive. Keep positive people around you and within your circle of people. Shortly after completing the photo shoot, God sent me another sign I was on the right path. Ms. Mitchell from Canada contacted me about speaking at their annual Trustee's Black History Event. I met Ms. Mitchell at the NABSE (National Alliance for Black School Educators) Conference about five years ago. We talked and exchanged contact information. El-Roy and I were presenting at NABSE that year. She attended our presentation, was impressed and stated then she was going to have me come talk in her school district. We would keep in touch over the years and connect at the conference each year. An opportunity presented itself and she contacted me to be the keynote speaker at their 2019 Trustee's Black History Event. I was beyond excited but had to play it semi-cool until that airfare and hotel confirmation was confirmed. When they did, once again, I looked up and thanked God. I connected with Sylus and his partner Yolanda to produce an introduction video I would use when speaking at the event. I traveled to Toronto, Canada. While there I visited Ms. Mitchell's school, spoke to her second grade classroom, teachers, staff and administration. I happened to look up the NBA (National Basketball Association) schedule before I left for Toronto and saw the Boston Celtics were playing the Toronto Raptors in Toronto that evening. Anybody that knows me knows I am a die-hard Boston Celtics fan. I ended up taking a cab to the game that evening to see the Celtics play the Raptors in Toronto. I bought a ticket from a ticket scalper outside the arena for $60. I mainly wanted to go to say I saw the Celtics play internationally. The arena and atmosphere was great overall.

Ms. Mitchell arranged for me to meet with Trustee Smith the following day at the Toronto School Board District Office. He invited Executive Superintendent Falconer. I spoke with each briefly about my work in Chicago aligned to increasing student achievement, specifically with black students. They shared their blueprint toward excellence in education of black students. Executive Superintendent Falconer was so impressed she invited me to speak to the other district superintendents who were having a meeting in a nearby boardroom. I spoke to them for about thirty minutes then opened up the session for questions. It was then once again, I had confirmation that I can do this work of increasing student achievement and building the capacity of others for overall school improvement. After the meeting and lunch, Ms. Mitchell arranged for me to speak to Ms. McLean, Equity Vice President of Toronto Education Workers. We talked for a while about our work and me coming back to present in Toronto and attend their annual conference which addresses equity in the workplace. Everyone I met on that trip was polite and welcoming. I look forward to working with the Toronto School district on increasing student achievement, specifically for black students and increasing equity in their school district. All of this was a result of effective networking. Yeah, I have the skill set and ability to articulate but it was who I knew, Ms. Mitchell that arranged the opportunity for me to exhibit those skills.

Upon my arrival back to the United States of America, I went back to my normal work schedule. Over that weekend, I received an email invite titled Safety Meeting – Mandatory at one of our schools. In summary, I had to put on my student advocate hat and inform the organizer that we needed to act in the best interest of the students. Fast forward: we would spend an entire two weeks at the school, analyzing their systems and structures and making recommendations for improvement while progress monitoring the changes put in place. I was not present at the school one day and upon my return, I learned we had not acted in the best interest of two students as a school district. I was livid and admittedly against the decision, yet, I was charged with being a part of the meeting to inform the parents. Just as I predicted, both parents were pissed. This was around the time another well-known Chicago Public Schools employee was released and/ or resigned and it was stated we must follow policy and uphold standards at all times. That was ironic.

At this time, I still hadn't received communication from the district about a possible transition meeting date and time or my next steps towards moving into a high school Chief of Schools position so I began to look at vacancies around the country that aligned to my instructional leadership skill set. I felt like the district left me no choice as there was so much uncertainty with the upcoming mayoral election and no clear outlook as it related to my pathway with the district. If I had received communication saying look you "f----d up, you need to improve in this area and we are going to gradually move you back up," I would have been fine that but the only communication I received was when the current Chief Education Officer said "we value Jeffery Dase" at the August 2018 Board of Education Meeting. What reassurance do I have that you truly value me if you are not willing to talk to me or provide me clarity aligned to my professional growth? So as I was looking at positions, each week on-line, I received a text message from one of my mentors, Dr. Constance Collins, about an assistant superintendent position posted for Decatur, Illinois. She texted me to send her names of anyone that may be a good fit for the position. I read the position criteria and decided to apply for myself. The search firm reviewed my application information and called me in for an interview. The interview went well. I felt like I answered all the questions with good articulation and content, and gave the impression I have expertise in the areas. I didn't feel good about my consistent energy in the interview, and when they asked me if I had any questions, I asked about my energy portrayed and it was like a light bulb went off as if they were excited I asked that question. They basically told me I was coming off as half dead and my energy was up and down throughout the interview. If I hadn't asked that question, I don't think I would have made it to the second interview. They couldn't give me feedback, but they were able to answer my question and I strongly feel the self-awareness impressed them.

I made it to the second round of interviews and made sure to keep my energy level up throughout the interview. We even had moments of laughter, which was good. I answered the questions to the best of my knowledge and articulated well. It felt like a conversation. The very last question was about the current curriculum and I answered honestly as I hadn't reviewed the current curriculum because I needed to talk to the teachers and students and other stakeholders along with reviewing the current curriculum prior to making an authentic assessment. I think they respected my honesty. The next day, the superintendent called me and asked me how I thought I did. I told him I think I did well overall but that there were some areas of improvement I immediately picked up on. He said I really impressed the committee and he would like to invite me back to walk the district and talk to him. Once again, I'm amazed at myself and it's all surreal for me. I went back to Decatur on the following Wednesday. Somehow I missed my turn off I-57 South to I-72 West and it placed me 30 minutes out the way. Luckily, I left early to allow time for any mishaps such as this one. Lesson. I eventually made it to Decatur at about 11:30 a.m. and read a couple of articles on the superintendent and checked in at the district office at 12:05 p.m., 10 minutes early for our scheduled 12:15 p.m. meeting time. Lesson learned. Superintendent Fregeau gave me an overview of the day's schedule and introduced me to his cabinet members before we headed out for the day. We visited two high schools, two middle schools and two elementary schools before heading back to the district office.

While we were out, we were discussing my work in Chicago and his work in Decatur, along with some personal conversation content like his family, my family and sports. We went back to his office where he would ask me a series of questions aligned to my resume content. He opened the floor to me for any questions and I asked him a series of questions about supporting my work as it would not be easy to apply the necessary changes from what I saw on our brief walk of the schools that day, diversity in the school district and in leadership positions and other questions about the position overall. I felt Superintendent Fregeau was extremely honest and transparent which was a quality I was looking for in a supervisor, leader, superintendent and partner. We finished our question and answer session and headed to dinner at a local steak house called The Gin Mill. I immediately felt the cost of living difference from Chicago when we were able to order a steak dinner with two sides for $34. Nowhere in Chicago is that possible especially for the quality of steak and service we received. He asked me how did I feel about the position now and I told him before I visited that day I was at a 7, now I was at a 9.5. I told him I was at a 9.5 because I felt like we "clicked" and that he was open, honest, and transparent and would support my work as the change that needed to take place was not going to make everyone happy. I then asked him what he was looking for in an assistant superintendent and he told me someone who will have the grit and fortitude to stay the course and do what needs to be done to move the school district forward. He said he did not want a yes man and he needed someone who would push him and his thinking as well. By the time we finished dinner and talking, I probably was at an 11 as it related to the position. I was scheduled to stay the night in Decatur but I told him that I had so much adrenaline from the possibility of being his assistant superintendent that I could make it home off of that and would drive home that night. I ended up cancelling my reservations at the hotel and drove home to Chicago that night. Those two hours went by quick. I was excited. I couldn't sleep that entire night. That night was filled with mixed emotions from excitement to bitterness as I was excited about my blessing and joining Decatur school district which was affirmation from God but bitter that I had to leave the district to acquire this affirmation.

This meant leaving my family, leaving my home, leaving my roots. This was not a slam dunk decision by far. Once again, I let go and let God deal with it. I had already declared a vacation day for the following day so I took a vacation day and meet with my IMPACT Mentor earlier in the day. The purpose of the meeting was to review my Hogan Assessment results. I would recommend this assessment to anyone in leadership, absolutely amazing. As we are reviewing my Hogan Assessment results, about 30 minutes in, my phone vibrates and I can see it is Superintendent Fregeau calling. Now, prior to this and reviewing my Hogan Assessment, I gave my mentor an overview of the process so she knew I was expecting the call that would tell me whether or not he selected me as the candidate. I answered the phone and she was smiling from ear to ear across the table from me. Dr. Fregeau tells me he would like to offer me the position. As I was talking, my mentor caught on that I was the one, and she started to literally cheer out loud. It was a priceless moment.

I got off the phone, we cheered and hugged each other and she says, okay, the hell with this, we will get to this later. Congratulations!

Before we ended the call I'd told Superintendent Fregeau naturally I'm excited and I want to talk to my mother, father and daughter. He understood and asked if I could let him know my answer by Sunday as he wanted to announce at the board meeting on the following Tuesday. That's when I asked him could he please not use my name for at least two weeks which would give me enough time to inform my current district leaders as I wanted to transition in the best professional way possible. He called back shortly and said he talked to the attorney and he said he could delay using my name until I sign the contract which would be three weeks from then which was perfect. I had already drafted a meeting request email to senior leadership requesting a transition meeting. I figured this would give me an opportunity to inform them face to face and if they ignored the request AGAIN then that would be my official closure to the request. Surprisingly, I received a response and meeting invite the next day. From the response, I'm wondering if it was a result of my including the district Chief Executive Officer on the email because the response stated she did not ever receive a written or verbal request for a meeting.

Thank you for reaching out to request a meeting to address your continued growth in the district. I would like to extend a sincere apology that you have not had a formal meeting after three requests. A formal meeting should have been scheduled at your request. This is unacceptable and does not align with the district and CEO's vision for customer service. However, for clarification purposes, please be advised that CEO ██████ has never received a written or verbal meeting request. I will take full responsibility for scheduling your requested transition meeting within the next week. Chief ██████ will also be in attendance and prepared to provide a summarized performance report, feedback and answer any outstanding questions that you may have related to your past and current role in the Office of Network Support. We value the contribution of every employee in CPS and look forward to addressing any concerns that you may have. Please expect to receive a meeting invite shortly.

I found that odd as my mentor had mentioned in August 2018 that she would be included in the transition meeting so from the response, I assumed she had no knowledge of my initial request

I would begin formalizing my questions for the scheduled meeting. In the meantime, I had to discuss the possible move to Decatur with my family. My mother was supportive. My dad was supportive as usual. The hard one was my daughter, Jakia. She initially shook her head in disagreement, but with more explanation and background, she gave me her approval and blessing. Her mother had called while I was telling her and she paused the conversation with her mother and asked me could she tell her. I said yes and she unmuted the telephone and said to her mother "now I'm not going to have any parent here." I was crushed inside. Her mother had moved to Virginia after she graduated from college. Now I was talking about moving so I can only imagine how she felt. I have invested twenty-three years of my life ensuring the best for her, so no position or amount of money was worth derailing that success. I truly required her blessing to make this move. After I left her house that night, I began strategizing on who would be on my support team to ensure my child was supported through this transition and beyond. I immediately called Shandrea. She responded "I got you!" I would ask Jakia one more time if I truly had her blessing before I called Superintendent Fregeau to inform him I would accept the position. She gave me her blessing and approval. I called Superintendent Fregeau and informed him of my conversation with my family and that I officially accepted the offer to be his Assistant Superintendent of Teaching and Learning. This was not only a blessing but it set a precedent and model for male leaders who are mostly seen as only culture and climate experts, not instructional leaders in the field of education. This was a victory for all future and aspiring male instructional leaders, not just black males. I have to give credit again to my mentor, Dr. Karen Saffold, who made the bold decision to place me with Chief of Schools Randel Josserand who was committed to using my instructional leadership and giving me autonomy to make a positive impact beyond my job title. He supported me through the process of my transition and the process of acquiring a position aligned to my instructional leadership skill set. This was possible with the support of Anthony Spivey and Eugene Crawford along with my inaugural Network Operations Manager colleagues, Dr. Daena Adams, Gabriela Reyes and Erin Washington. I missed a lot of days and meetings with my IMPACT Leadership classes and pursuing the assistant superintendent position but they did not ever waver in their support and encouragement. I am forever grateful to them all.

On April 5, 2019, I finally received the transition meeting I had been requesting since July 2018, 253 days later since my infamous transition meeting. The meeting was attended by my mentor and former boss. There was a prepared agenda and data on the table at the beginning of the meeting. They allowed me to state my purpose for the meeting and I simply asked for a rationale as to why I was transitioned from the Chief of Schools position and if the plan was to transition me into a high school Chief of Schools position, why hasn't the professional development or communication been present. It was a similar meeting to the last meeting I had with my former boss only this time she admitted to not communicating effectively with me and that she could have done a better job of providing me with examples of my so-called areas of development. Honestly, I was pleased at that moment and could have left and been satisfied but my mentor began telling me all these stories about what principals were saying about me as Chief of Schools. Some of these stories were from principals that were not even in my network. If she told me ten stories, I was aware of only two. I asked her the question, how would I address these issues if I knew nothing about them? Most of the alleged issues I was just finding out about at this meeting, however, as my mentor with 24/7 access to me, I had no communication about these issues from my mentor or boss. I had nothing else to say to either my mentor or former boss but respected my former boss for acknowledging her shortcomings as my supervisor.

I informed them I was pursuing positions outside the school district. After 22 years with the Chicago Public Schools district, going above and beyond as a tutor, teacher, assistant principal, principal, Chief of Schools, not to mention a black male advancing in these positions with data to show I was successful in every position I held with the school district, the woman I held higher than all because she made me told me I was transitioned from my Chief of Schools position because of what others were saying about me. Needless to say, I was crushed again because that's how much I valued her voice and opinion. I reflected on that meeting over the weekend and realized we did not discuss my data at all during the meeting, which was unfortunate, because that would have been a highlight. I used the content of the meeting as learning and fuel to leave no possibility in the future. The Lord spoke to me through my new Assistant Superintendent contract with contract item 11 which states "The Board collectively and individually and the Superintendent shall promptly refer all criticisms, complaints, and suggestions called to its/ their attention to the Assistant Superintendent for study and recommendations."

If only my mentor and former boss would have had that guidance and followed through, I guarantee I would have remained Chief of Schools for Chicago Public Schools. The Lord also spoke to me when I was transitioned as He gave me another life lesson and test, don't rely solely on people, rely on HIM. Everything I went through this past year was to prepare me for my next glorious journey in helping God's children, only this time, the bulk of that help will go towards the students of Decatur, Illinois. My time in Chicago as an official Chicago Public Schools educator expired on June 30, 2019 at 11:59 p.m.

My next chapter of greatness began in Decatur Public Schools on July 1, 2019 at 12:00 a.m. I'm back home as an instructional leader.

This is a testimony, when presented with obstacles, let it go and let God handle it. Thank you, Lord.

From Church Street to the Chief Seat,

Now the Assistant Superintendent Seat

jeffdase181@gmail.com

Social Media: @jeffdase

CONCLUSION

"The weak can never forgive. Forgiveness is the attribute of the strong." –Mahatma Gandhi

"When a deep injury is done to us, we never heal until we forgive." –Nelson Mandela

"Mistakes are always forgivable, if one has the courage to admit them." –Bruce Lee

"To be a Christian means to forgive the inexcusable because God has forgiven the inexcusable in you." –C.S. Lewis

"Forgiveness is a reflection of loving yourself enough to move on." –Dr. Steve Maraboli

"Forgiveness is not always easy. At times it feels more painful than the wound we suffered, to forgive the one that inflicted it. And yet, there is no peace without forgiveness."
-Marianne Williamson

"Forgiveness is the final form of love." –Reinhold Niebuhr

Writing this book has given me added strength and has been therapy for my soul. I have battled with psychological injuries inflicted mostly by those that have been close to me. I don't ask anybody to do anything I am not willing to do myself and I am not perfect. I have made mistakes. I have sought forgiveness. I forgive all those that have trespassed against me. I have survived the pain so I thank them for making me a stronger human being. No one wants to experience pain but making it through is rewarding in itself. For every person that has inflicted pain in my life, the Lord has blessed my life with another person or people to help me cope or heal that pain. Writing this book has allowed me to assess my inner self. The psychological pain has not been easy to deal with, however it has provided me motivation to LOVE even more. I LOVE those that have trespassed against me – past, present and future. – **Jeff Dase**

Made in the
USA
Lexington, KY